FRUITFUL DISCIPLESHIP

LIVING THE MISSION OF JESUS IN THE CHURCH AND THE WORLD

Sherry A. Weddell

Our Sunday Visitor

www.osv.com
Our Sunday Visitor Publishing Division
Our Sunday Visitor, Inc.
Huntington, Indiana 46750

Our Sunday Visitor Publishing Division, Our Sunday Visitor, Inc., 200 Noll Plaza, Huntington, IN 46750; 1-800-348-2440

ISBN: 978-1-61278-973-6 (Inventory No. T1734)
eISBN: 978-1-61278-974-3
LCCN: 2017936923

Cover design: Lindsey Riesen
Cover photo: Shutterstock
Interior design: Dianne Nelson

PRINTED IN THE UNITED STATES OF AMERICA

ABOUT THE AUTHOR

Sherry Weddell created the first charism-discernment process for Catholics in 1993 and co-founded the Catherine of Siena Institute (CSI) in 1997 with Father Michael Sweeney, O.P. The Institute trains Catholic leaders in the art of twenty-first-century evangelization and fostering parishes of intentional missionary disciples, in facilitating the discernment of charisms and vocations among all the baptized, and in the theology, formation, and mission of the laity. Sherry and her international team of collaborators have worked directly with 140,000 lay, religious, and ordained Catholics in well over 500 parishes in 150 dioceses across North America and in Europe, Asia, and Oceania.

Sherry is the author of *Forming Intentional Disciples: The Path to Knowing and Following Jesus* (2012) (also available in Spanish as *Formación de Discípulos Intencionales* and in Polish as *Badz Uczniem Jezusa*). She also edited and contributed to *Forming a Parish of Intentional Disciples* (2015). When Sherry is not hanging out in airports, she enjoys tending her high-altitude Tuscan garden in the Colorado Rockies.

By this is my Father glorified,
that you bear much fruit
and become my disciples.
John 15:8

CONTENTS

ACKNOWLEDGMENTS

INTRODUCTION

One of the greatest blessings of my life over the past two decades has been the opportunity to listen to tens of thousands of Catholics around the world describe how God is using them in the lives of others. The one-on-one listening sessions that we call *gifts interviews* are just about the most fun you can have legally. We hear these words over and over: "I've never told anyone this story before but...."

For my collaborators and me, the interviews have provided a stunning window into the realities of God's grace at work in our world that regular Catholics in the pews hardly ever get the chance to put into words. The stories we've heard run the gamut from the funny to the unexpected to the hopeful, and occasionally to the gloriously extraordinary. (I once had the chance to listen to someone describe an experience of bilocation!)

Of course, the experience of the vast majority of those we have helped to discern charisms is more mainstream but just as moving. You don't have to appear exceptional to the world to be used in remarkable ways by God. As St. Teresa of Kolkata observed: "[Jesus] will use you to accomplish great things on the condition that you believe much more in his love than in your weakness. Only then, his hand will be free with you."[1]

This book was written for the same audience for which I wrote *Forming Intentional Disciples* — the "Core," the Catholic leaders, ordained and lay, at all levels of the Church's life whose

---

[1] The first sentence of the quote is from Mother Teresa, "Jesus Christ: He wants to love with our hearts and serve with our hands" (online at http://www.vatican.va/jubilee_2000/magazine/documents/ju_mag_01031997_p-10_en.html, as of May 5, 2017); the second sentence is from Mother Teresa, *No Greater Love* (Novato, CA: New World Library, 2002), p. 87.

vision and decisions will determine our future. But this is *not* the Called & Gifted workshop in book form.

That's because the discernment and exercise of the charisms is just one part of the larger and more fundamental issue of fruitfulness: the manifestation of God's power, purposes, and provision in history through the intentional cooperation of disciples with grace. The world and the whole human race is waiting for the fruit that you and I have been anointed by the Holy Spirit to bear, and the charisms are just one important kind of fruit.

We *have* learned an enormous amount over the past twenty-three years about how to help Catholic adults of all ages and backgrounds discern and answer the call of God that comes with a charism. What I didn't understand was how little of that accumulated savvy you can cram into a book of manageable size. I worked hard to cover the most basic principles, but I need to make it clear that reading this book is neither the equivalent of going through an actual discernment process nor does it include the *Catholic Spiritual Gifts Inventory*. (If you would like to go through a discernment process, please visit the Catherine of Siena Institute website at www.siena.org and give us the chance to assist you.)

I owe an enormous debt to our Institute staff and our indefatigable traveling and regional teachers and trainers, who make it possible for me to take time off the road, and to the 140,000 Catholics who have shared their experiences of God with us over the past twenty years. It has been a tremendous privilege to collaborate with the thousands of Catholic leaders: bishops, pastors, diocesan and parish staff, and so many others who have worked with us to foster the missionary discipleship and discernment of Catholics over the years. In the writing of this book, I am especially beholden to the apostolic passion and hard-won wisdom of Katherine Coolidge, Bobby Vidal, Father Michael Sweeney, O.P., Mark and Janet Shea, Deacon Keith Strohm, Dave VanVickle, Sherry Curp, Gary Weddell, Cindy Cavnar, Craig Pohl, Jennifer Brown, Bishop Earl Boyea, Father Tom Firestone, Father James Mangan, and all the priests and leaders of the Flint Catholic Community.

I can't end without a shout-out to the 7,200 members of the Forming Intentional Disciples Facebook Forum. Being able to pick the brains and receive the prayers of some of the most astute and effective Catholic evangelizers from around the world at a moment's notice has been incredibly fruitful and encouraging. It is the ultimate twenty-first-century Catholic evangelizer's brain trust and support network. Our experience on the Forum has shown that we can use social media to duplicate some of the collaborative dynamics of the Generation of Saints who were the catalysts of the great Catholic revival in early seventeenth-century France.

Blessed be God in all his gifts!

CHAPTER 1

The Weight of My Neighbor's Glory

All of us, gazing with unveiled face on the glory of the Lord, are being transformed into the same image from glory to glory, as from the Lord who is the Spirit.

2 CORINTHIANS 3:18

There is a story that I love to tell at every Called & Gifted workshop that I teach: the extraordinary life of Margaret Haughery, the bread saint of New Orleans.

Margaret was born in Ireland but lived most of her life in New Orleans. By the time she was twenty-three, Margaret's parents, husband, and infant daughter had all died. She was penniless, uneducated, and alone. Although she originally supported herself as a laundress, Margaret quickly began to start businesses. She first founded a dairy and peddled the milk door-to-door. She used the money she made to buy a bankrupt bakery and turned it around, becoming enormously successful. The penniless orphan made a fortune and gave almost all of it away.

A devout Catholic, she lived a life of great simplicity — she owned only two dresses at a time. She was known as the "mother of orphans" because, for decades, she made and gave away vast sums to feed the poor, while founding and supporting homes for orphans and widows of all backgrounds.

Margaret's wisdom was proverbial. Seated in the doorway of her famous bakery, she was consulted by people of all ranks. When she died in 1882, she was given a state funeral and all New Orleans mourned. What I find most moving is that the plain but fabulous Irish social entrepreneur that everyone called "our Margaret" did all this without ever learning to read or write.[1]

Margaret Haughery is a perfect example of why I love this observation by A. D. Lindsay:

> The difference between ordinary people and saints is not that saints fulfill the plain duties that ordinary men neglect. The things saints do have not usually occurred to ordinary people at all.... "Gracious" conduct is like the work of an artist. It needs imagination and spontaneity. It is not the choice between presented alternatives but the creation of something new.[2]

Which brings me to the point of this book.

The greatest riches of the Church are not found in our gorgeous legacy of art and architecture, our brilliant philosophical and scientific heritage, or even our nearly 700,000 institutions that currently serve the dignity and eternal destiny of human beings on this planet. All of these treasures, wonderful and critical as they are, are *fruit* borne by human beings who, like the unlikely Margaret Haughery, freely responded to and cooperated with the grace of God in their time and place. Our

---

[1] "Margaret Haughery," *Wikipedia* (online at https://en.wikipedia.org/wiki/Margaret_Haughery , as of May 5, 2017).

[2] A. D. Lindsay, "The Two Moralities," quoted in Dorothy L. Sayers, *The Whimsical Christian* (New York: Collier, 1987), p. 131.

greatest earthly treasures are our Margarets: the 1.272 billion immortals and potential fruit-bearers who currently bear the surname "Catholic."[3]

As C. S. Lewis observed:

> There are no ordinary people. You have never talked to a mere mortal. Nations, cultures, arts, civilizations — these are mortal, and their life is to ours as the life of a gnat. But it is immortals whom we joke with, work with, marry, snub and exploit — immortal horrors or everlasting splendors.[4]

Pope St. John Paul II understood this deeply:

> ... God with his call reaches the heart of each individual, and the Spirit, who abides deep within each disciple (cf. 1 Jn 3:24), gives himself to each Christian with different charisms and special signs. Each one, therefore, must be helped to embrace the gift entrusted to him as a completely unique person, and to hear the words which the Spirit of God personally addresses to him.[5]

No wonder the Church insists that "the ministerial priesthood is at the service of the common priesthood. It is

---

[3] St. Pacian famously observed in a letter, "Christian is my name, but Catholic my surname": "Letter 1: On the Catholic Name," 7, in *The Extant Works of St. Pacian, Library of Fathers of the Holy Catholic Church* 17 (1842), pp. 317-327 (online at http://www.tertullian.org/fathers/pacian_1_letter1.htm, as of May 5, 2017).

[4] C. S. Lewis, *The Weight of Glory* (New York: HarperCollins, 2001), p. 46.

[5] Pope St. John Paul II, *Pastores Dabo Vobis* ("I Will Give You Shepherds"), 40 (online at http://w2.vatican.va/content/john-paul-ii/en/apost_exhortations /documents/hf_jp-ii_exh_25031992_pastores-dabo-vobis.html, as of May 5, 2017).

directed at the *unfolding of the baptismal grace of all Christians*" (*Catechism of the Catholic Church* [CCC] 1547, emphasis added).

WHERE'S THE FRUIT?

The question "Where's the fruit?" is one that I've been asking for years. A lot of Catholic leaders are asking the same question. For instance, the leadership of a Catholic university brought me in after reading my book *Forming Intentional Disciples: The Path to Knowing and Following Jesus.* They said, "We have a problem. We thought that if we exposed our students to *thick* Catholic culture — the very best of Catholic liturgies, music, art, literature, philosophy, and theology — they would naturally become disciples and behave like disciples. But it's not working. We're realizing that we actually have to evangelize our students and explicitly call them to discipleship."

One of the inevitable results of our failure to evangelize and make intentional disciples of our own is that so many of the graces Catholics have objectively received are not bearing their intended fruit. We can learn a lot from the powerful little two-paragraph section of the *Catechism* entitled "Liturgy as Source of Life":

1071 ... [The liturgy] involves the "conscious, active, and *fruitful* participation" of everyone. (emphasis added)

1072 "The sacred liturgy does not exhaust the entire activity of the Church": *it must be preceded by evangelization, faith, and conversion. It can then produce its fruits in the lives of the faithful: new life in the Spirit, involvement in the mission of the Church, and service to her unity.* (emphasis added)

Where do we stand in terms of fruit-bearing? I will not make you wade through a mass of depressing statistics; a few quick snapshots will do.

In 2014, 6.5 American Catholics left the Church for every non-Catholic who entered, and half of millennials (ages 18-34) raised Catholic have already dropped the identity.[6] I asked pastors and catechists in a dozen different dioceses this past fall how many of the children and teens in their confirmation prep programs had stopped attending Mass since they were confirmed. The estimates that I received ranged from 60 to 90 percent. Millions of young adults raised in the Church and then simply vanishing do not qualify as "fruit."

Fruit-bearing is the canary in our ecclesial coal mine. It is the most critical external evidence we have that we are doing — or not doing — what Jesus commanded us to do: Make disciples of all nations. The truth is that acceptance of little or no fruit as "normal" has profoundly shaped the lives of almost all Catholics as well as our pastoral practice, our vocational discernment, and our mission to the world.

What is the abundant fruit, which God is calling us to bear? What are the consequences of our failure to make disciples, and to help those disciples grow to fruit-bearing maturity? What hangs in the balance?

- The eternal happiness in God — the salvation — of every human being on the planet.
- Lavish, life-changing, and culture-changing fruitfulness, pouring out into the world through the lives of the faithful.
- The emergence of the next generations of Catholic leaders, saints, and apostles: priestly, religious, and secular. And through them ...

---

[6] *America's Changing Religious Landscape*, Pew Research Center (May 12, 2015), pp. 35 and 41 (online at http://www.pewforum.org/2015/05/12 /americas-changing-religious-landscape/, as of May 5, 2017).

- The fulfillment of the Church's mission and the redemptive work of Jesus Christ in history.

The Virtue of Faith and the Act of Faith

Which brings us to the ancient distinction between what the Church calls the *virtus fidei* and the *actus fidei*. *Virtus fidei* is the "virtue of faith," the power or capacity to believe given to us by God in valid baptism. When you read in the *Catechism* or magisterial documents that baptism bestows faith, the document is referring to the *virtue* of faith.

But the *actus fidei*, the "act of faith," is different. This is the explicit, personal, free choice of an older child or adult to *respond* to God's grace with belief and discipleship, to embark upon what St. Paul called the "obedience of faith" (Romans 1:5). *Actus fidei* is where the rubber hits the road and we *do* what we say we believe. Evangelization addresses this question: Have we made a personal "act of faith"? It is the *personal act of faith* that is the key to bearing fruit.

THE SEEKER JOURNEY

At the Catherine of Siena Institute, we have long used a very simple schema to help participants in our Making Disciples seminars understand the developmental process that adults typically go through in the twenty-first century West as they move toward intentional discipleship. We call them the Seeker, Disciple, and Apostle stages of spiritual development.

The Seeker stage corresponds to the long pre-discipleship journey from distrust and disbelief to what the *Catechism* calls a person's "first and fundamental conversion" (CCC 1427), the point where you drop your nets and begin to follow

Jesus consciously as his disciple in the midst of his Church. Depending upon where they start, some people have a long way to travel before they arrive at that crossroads.

The Seeker stage encompasses the five thresholds of conversion that I cover in considerable detail in chapters 5 through 8 of *Forming Intentional Disciples*.[7] The thresholds have to do with our *lived relationship* with God, not our religious background or lack of it. In brief, the five thresholds are:

1. Initial Trust
2. Spiritual Curiosity
3. Spiritual Openness
4. Spiritual Seeking
5. Intentional Discipleship[8]

Trust. In the post-modern West, the vast majority of non-practicing or non-believing Christians, as well as people from non-Christian or "nothing" backgrounds, have to start with some positive association with Christianity, with Christ, or with a believing Christian. They need a bridge of *trust* in place across which they can move closer to Christ and his Church. If there is no bridge of trust in place, then the first task of an evangelizer is to *build* or *become* a relational bridge of personal and spiritual trust that can one day bear the weight of truth.

Curiosity. After trust has been established, the next development stage is spiritual *curiosity*. As disciple-makers, we want to foster curiosity about the person and work of Jesus Christ rather than about a generic "faith" or simply factual

---

7   This is a very brief review. To learn more about the thresholds, please see chapters 5-8 of *Forming Intentional Disciples: The Path to Knowing and Following Jesus* (Huntington, IN: Our Sunday Visitor, 2012).

8   Adapted from "Five Thresholds of Postmodern Evangelism," by Doug Schaupp, 1998 (online at http://www.illinoisgcf.org/execplanning/resources /FiveThresholdsPaper.pdf, as of May 5, 2017).

questions about Catholic beliefs and practices. If we do not intentionally foster curiosity about Jesus as the center of our faith, people can (and do) easily come away with the impression that Catholicism is primarily about an institution rather than a relationship to the person of Jesus, Lord of the Church, who came, lived, died, and rose again for us.

Openness. As that curiosity builds, the seeker becomes *open* to the possibility of personal and spiritual change, which is a big turning point. Openness is not a *commitment* to change, just the willingness to acknowledge to God and to yourself that you are open to the *possibility* of change. Since to do so involves giving up the sense of having absolute control over one's own life and dropping one's defenses, it can feel scary and even absolutely crazy. People typically need support from others as they move into openness.

Seeking. The next stage is spiritual *seeking*, where people are now actively grappling with whether or not they will choose to follow Jesus as his disciple in the midst of his Church. Consider this Gospel story:

> As he was walking by the Sea of Galilee, he saw two brothers, Simon who is called Peter, and his brother Andrew, casting a net into the sea; they were fishermen. He said to them, "Come after me, and I will make you fishers of men." At once they left their nets and followed him. (Matthew 4:18-20)

The spiritual *seeker*, like Peter and Andrew, is holding his or her nets — his or her entire life — and is steadily regarding Jesus and *thinking* about whether to drop those nets and follow him. The spiritual seeker has *not* yet dropped his or her net to follow Jesus but is grappling with whether to do so. It is a time of intense spiritual reflection that feels, for many, like a quest.

Intentional Disciple. Finally, we come to the moment that people do drop their nets and cross the last threshold to begin the life of an *intentional disciple*. Some are finally responding with faith to the baptismal graces they had received as an infant; others make this journey consciously as teens or adults before baptism. For instance, Cornelius the Centurion, seeking to know the way of salvation, sends for Peter to hear his message and experiences conversion *before* baptism (see Acts 10:44-48).

MISSIONARY DISCIPLE:
FOLLOWING JESUS AND BEING SENT BY JESUS

The developmental stage of *disciple* corresponds to what the *Catechism* calls the "second conversion" (CCC 1428), a lifelong conversion. A man or woman who is now seeking to follow Jesus as a disciple grows spiritually and is transformed as he or she walks with Christ.

Catechesis really comes into its own as disciples become excited and eagerly want to learn more about the faith. They begin to grow in virtue as they integrate not only Catholic doctrine but also the basic disciplines of discipleship into their work, their relationships and family life, their recreation, and so on. Not only do their personal lives change, but they begin to actively cooperate with and be used by God for others. As disciples mature, they start to feel strong enough to go public with their faith, even in situations where people are indifferent or hostile to Christianity.

In a word, the Disciple stage is where people start to *bear fruit* because their priorities change from within. They want to worship, so they attend Mass regularly. They pray and ask to be taught how to pray. They are eager to serve. Many disciples become the backbone of their local parishes because they care so much about the well-being of the Church. They become good stewards of their finances out of a passion to see the Gospel advance and change other people's lives. Evangelizing parishes regularly tell us that they have the highest *per capita* giving in their diocese.

Disciples will fill every class in your parish and diocese because they long to study and grow in the faith. They clamor to discern how God is calling them. Their charisms — special graces of the Holy Spirit that empower us to be a channel of God's beauty, mercy, provision, truth, and healing for others — become manifest in their lives. They are eager to pass their faith on to their children and are no longer willing to just drop them off at sacramental prep before spending an hour killing time with their phone and a latte. Now they are serious, active collaborators who passionately embrace their roles as the primary catechists in the lives of their children.

All of this and so much more that we desperately want to see happen in our parishes starts to emerge, not out of guilt, but out of a living, growing relationship with God. It bursts out as naturally as apples on apple trees — and for the same reason: every one of these things is the *fruit* Jesus promises his disciples will bear: "fruit that will remain" (John 15:16).

THE APOSTLE STAGE

In Church teaching, there are important differences between what is called "objective" redemption and "subjective" redemption. By his life, death, and resurrection, Jesus has already reconciled us with the Father: this is *objective* redemption. *Subjective* redemption is the *application* of the saving gifts of Christ to individuals, the manifestation of salvific transformation in each of our lives. Human beings contribute nothing to the work of Christ in objective redemption, but the exercise of our free cooperation with God's grace is *central* in the drama of subjective redemption.

As disciples mature, they reach a turning point where they take personal ownership and responsibility for the mission of the Church. They realize that they have also been anointed and sent by Christ on a mission, and that there is no such thing as missional unemployment for the baptized. They have entered the *Apostle* stage of development. Apostles know that they also are one of the Lord's "sent ones" or in Pope Francis' memorable phrase: "*missionary disciples*."[9] They grasp that every one of us has a vocation: a work of love to which we have been called by God, and through which he is going to change us and change the world around us.

The Apostle stage of spiritual development is where people discern their personal vocations and abundant fruit-bearing becomes the *norm*. This is where lay apostles engage in both challenging the societal structures of sin and helping to create new structures ordered toward redemption and the flourishing of human beings. This is the developmental stage where Catholics become passionate about the active evangelization of those who do not yet know Christ and his Church.

THE END FOR WHICH WE LABOR

In the end, all our pastoral and catechetical work is not just for the child being baptized and catechized but for the adult that child is called by God to become. The end for which we labor

---

[9] Pope Francis, *Evangelii Gaudium*, 120 (online at http://w2.vatican.va/content /francesco/en/apost_exhortations/documents/papa-francesco_esortazione -ap_20131124_evangelii-gaudium.html, as of May 5, 2017); cf. *Apostolicam Actuositatem* (Decree on the Apostolate of the Laity), 3 (online at http://www .vatican.va/archive/hist_councils/ii_vatican_council/documents/vat -ii_decree_19651118_apostolicam-actuositatem_en.html, as of May 5, 2017).

is the mature Christian who is both (1) an *immortal* intended for eternal happiness with God and (2) an *apostle* in his or her particular sphere — an agent of subjective redemption and abundant fruit-bearing through his or her cooperation with grace. We glorify God by facilitating the salvation and eternal happiness of immortals and the continual emergence of new missionary disciples who are actively encouraged to grow into the fullness of their earthly influence and creativity. It is these two ends that we serve when we evangelize and make disciples.

A FAMINE OF FRUIT

I have not found any research in this area, but I would like to share a very rough practitioner's working estimate. Based on our experience to date working with 140,000 Catholics in over 500 parishes in 150 dioceses in 12 countries, I estimate that perhaps 3 percent of all the individual charisms and individual vocations[10] that we have been given by God are being manifested and lived.

Christian vocation is a mystery that emerges from a sustained encounter with Jesus Christ. Because we are not yet calling most of our people to discipleship, their charisms and vocations are not manifesting, being discerned, and lived. Indeed, our failure to evangelize actually *suppresses the emergence of vocations* because the desire to discern God's call is one of the normal fruits of discipleship. As a result, both the Church and the world are starved for lack of the abundant fruit that the Body of Christ has been anointed to bear.

---

[10] The Church teaches about three basic kinds of vocation: (1) the universal vocation to holiness; (2) state-of-life vocations (priesthood, religious, marriage, singleness); and (3) individual, personal vocations. In addition to a "state of life" vocation, many are also given individual, personal vocations. So, a married mother of two may also have been given a vocation to serve as a physician or as an artist, etc.

How this has complicated the discernment process can be seen in the way ordinary lay Catholics so often assume that the term "vocation" refers only to priestly or religious vocation and is rare rather than universal. We expect a few people will be drawn out of the parish to go to the diocese, the seminary, or religious community because they have a special call. In practice, the rest of the laity remaining in the parish is presumed by nearly everyone to have nothing to discern. Therefore, no serious discernment support is made available for those who are not called to one of the obvious ecclesial vocations.

Recently, I spoke to a national gathering of religious vocation directors. I asked them, "How many of you have inquirers come to you who are not ready to discern?" The response was unanimous, "We all do." I responded that most Catholics assume that only very exceptional people embark on a personal spiritual quest. So, it is very easy for those who are just beginning to move into a new threshold like curiosity or openness to conclude that their new and apparently rare surge in spiritual interest must mean they are called to a *rare vocation*: priesthood or religious life.

My friend Janet is a good example. She was raised Catholic and experienced a serious conversion as a child. Growing up, she decided that she must be called to become a sister since religious life was the only place where she knew Catholics talked out loud about God.

Janet entered a women's community but eventually discerned that she was not called to religious life and left, still seeking God. For a time, she "double-dipped," dividing her time between attendance at Mass and participation in a small non-denominational evangelical church. Why? Because that little evangelical congregation strongly encouraged its members to lives of conscious discipleship, fostered the discernment of charisms, and surrounded her with love and support as she passionately sought to follow Jesus. Eventually, Jan married. When her husband became a fervent Catholic convert, she returned full-time to her life as a Catholic. Despite years of serious spiritual searching, Jan did not grasp — until she was in her thirties — that she could be a lay disciple *in the Catholic Church*.

No wonder the Church is struggling. The vast majority of those to whom the power of the Holy Spirit has been given are not yet manifesting that power. This is why what Pope St. John Paul II taught is so important:

> Therefore, the Church fulfills her mission when she guides every member of the faithful to discover and live his or her own vocation in freedom and to bring it to fulfillment in charity. [11]

MISSIONARY DISCIPLE IN THE MUSLIM WORLD

My oldest female friend (I'll call her "Natali") is an American who has lived for decades in a variety of Muslim countries. I first met Natali the day after I graduated from college and thought of her as a sophisticated "older" woman. After all, she was married and in her thirties with both a house and a profession. Over the next two years, we became good friends — and then she left to live in the Middle East.

Every summer since, we have gotten together when she returns to the States for vacation. Natali downloads her year with me in long, rich conversations, telling amazing stories of God at work in and through her relationships in some of the most complex and difficult places on earth.

Today, Natali would strike a stranger as a quite ordinary, five-foot-nuthin' wife, mother, and grandmother. And what a mistake that would be. She and her husband spent years

---

[11] Pope St. John Paul II, *Pastores Dabo Vobis*, 40.

equipping themselves to be "tent-making" missionaries — that is, Christians who (like St. Paul the tentmaker in Acts 18:3) work at a secular profession that enables them to live where no overt missionary work is possible so that some living witness to the love of Jesus Christ might be found there. She speaks the language fluently and has a real charism in this area. She frequently goes places where no Western women go and where she has developed many friendships. She is credible and approachable because she is a housewife and mother and so can connect with the other women who are also raising their families. With them, she not only shares goat and spiced coffee but the love of Jesus.

What she does is possible only because she is a layperson. No "official" missionary, no pastor, priest, or nun would be allowed into the country. No man would be allowed to enter the situations and relationships where she has been welcomed as a woman. My friend is supported in her efforts not only by her husband but also by her Protestant congregation back home and an international missionary organization.

When a lay Catholic embarks upon an apostolate outside the standard ecclesial structures in the United States, he or she usually has to carve out an individual, and often, quite lonely path. Lay Catholics serious about their secular mission usually have to be remarkably independent and persistent.

A few years ago, I taught a three-hour graduate class on the development of the Church's understanding of the laity from 1497 (St. Catherine of Genoa and the Oratory of Divine Love) to 1957, the year of the Second World Congress on the Apostolate of the Laity. I was trying to help my students grasp the experience of the Church regarding the laity over those 460 years, because that experience had shaped the bishops attending the Second Vatican Council and, therefore, the debate over the vocation, mission, and charisms of the laity that took place in October 1963.

My students were surprised to learn that Pope Pius XII had been a great champion of the term "lay apostle." In his address to the Second World Congress, Pope Pius XII referred to "lay apostles" twenty-three times. In fact, he observed that, in 1957, " *'lay apostle'* is one of the terms most widely used in discussing the activities of the Church."[12]

Five years earlier, in 1952, Pius XII had spoken of his intense desire for huge numbers of both priestly and lay apostles:

> We would love to have vast phalanxes of apostles rise up, like those that the Church knew at her origins ... and next to the priests, let the laity speak, who have learned to penetrate the minds and hearts of their listeners with their word and love. Yes, bearers of life, penetrate, in every place — in factories, workshops, fields — wherever Christ has the right to enter. Offer yourselves, see yourselves among your own kind, in diverse centers of work, in the same houses, closely and tightly united, in one thought and desire only. And then open wide your arms to welcome all who come to you, anxious for a helpful and reassuring word in this atmosphere of darkness and discomfort.[13]

The Pope was calling the laity to be magnanimous. The virtue of magnanimity is the aspiration to do great things, to bear great fruit for God and his Kingdom. Pope Pius XII knew that St. Thomas Aquinas called magnanimity the "ornament of

---

[12] Pope Pius XII, *Guiding Principles of the Lay Apostolate*, Second World Congress of the Lay Apostolate, October 5, 1957, emphasis added (online at https://www.ewtn.com/library/PAPALDOC/P12LAYAP.HTM, as of May 5, 2017).

[13] Pope Pius XII, *"Christians, Bearer of the Life of the Risen One,"* Homily for Easter Sunday, 1952, *Compendium on the New Evangelization* (United States Conference of Catholic Bishops, 2015), p. 14.

all the virtues."[14] The magnanimous person has the courage to seek out what is truly great and become worthy of it.

When I first encountered the idea that aspiring to this sort of holy greatness was considered to be a *virtue* by the Church, I had difficulty taking it in. *Saints* do great things for God. But aren't ordinary lay Catholics supposed to be humble and not presumptuous, to minimize our abilities and significance, and avoid big expectations?

As we have observed hundreds of times in the Called & Gifted discernment process, even the *idea* of having charisms and being anointed for a mission unnerves many lay Catholics, especially those who are older. Believing that God might do something genuinely important and supernatural through them seems to lack humility. Over and over in the course of helping laypeople discern their charisms, they have told me of their deep belief in the virtue of *living small and expecting little of God.* As one particularly charming eighty-four-year-old Scot told me in a lilting brogue, "I couldn't have charisms! It wouldn't be humble!"

We must recognize that humility is magnanimity's necessary partner, the attitude before God that recognizes and fully accepts our creaturehood and the immeasurable distance between the Creator and his creation. But in Catholic thought, humility never stands alone. Without magnanimity, we don't see the whole of our dignity as human beings. Magnanimity and humility *together* enable us to keep our balance, to arrive at our proper worth before God, to persist in living our mission, and to persevere in seeking our eternal destiny despite apparent frustration and failure.

---

[14] St. Thomas Aquinas, *Summa Theologiae*, II-II, q129, a4, Objection 3 (online at http://www.newadvent.org/summa/3129.htm, as of May 5, 2017).

C.S. Lewis captures perfectly the significance of the responsibility that all disciples bear for one another's development in this area:

It may be possible for each to think too much of his own potential glory hereafter; it is hardly possible for him to think too often or too deeply about that of his neighbor. The load, or weight, or burden of my neighbor's glory should be laid daily on my back, a load so heavy that only humility can carry it, and the backs of the proud will be broken. [15]

---

[15] Lewis, *The Weight of Glory*, p. 46.

CHAPTER 2

Where's the Fruit?

"By this is my Father glorified, that you bear much fruit and become my disciples."

JOHN 15:8

My friend "Bill" works in a Southeastern parish that recently went through yet another pastoral turnover. Bill has been the carrier of the evangelization-and-discipleship flame in his parish for years as pastors come and go. It is common practice in his diocese for members of the priest personnel board to meet with parish leadership to get a better sense of the community before making the decision about which priest to assign as pastor.

The parish's pastoral team — staff members, finance and pastoral council — prepped for the meeting. To help everyone focus, Bill outlined several specific areas of spiritual fruit that had emerged in their parish. Everyone was encouraged to pick one area and share a story that showed how their parish was moving from maintenance to mission.

As the parish leaders told their stories to the visiting board members, many were in tears. One woman talked about how she had once only felt capable of volunteering to make sandwiches for the homeless. After growing significantly in her relationship with Jesus, she felt called by Jesus to confront the city about opening a homeless shelter.

Another man told the story of some people visiting the parish who felt the Holy Spirit descend on them when they stepped onto the parish grounds. The visitors sensed that God was asking them to move to the parish from another state because of what he desired to do there. Others talked about how they were no longer afraid to have spiritual conversations with family members and strangers. Many talked about how the community needed to go out of the parish and learn how to better proclaim Jesus.

One person reported hearing from Protestant friends who said, "They have their eye on us." Another individual shared how she had left the Church and was hurt and upset with the Church. She attended Mass at the parish and was welcomed in an extraordinary way. As a result, she underwent a conversion, was discipled in the parish, and is now a staff member.

The stories went on and on. One of the visiting board members openly wept and said that she felt like she had just been on a retreat experience. Bill told me afterward that he did not have to say a single word.

Toward A Culture of Discipleship

Bill's story shows the remarkable changes that a parish and its people can experience when there are many disciples, and as a result, the culture of the whole parish changes. Significant fruit, even amazing fruit, is borne. People can't help but recognize the change.

I couldn't hide my own surprise a few years ago in front of the leaders of a parish in another part of the county who were also experiencing an extraordinary amount of fruit. I had to tell them: "You do realize this is not normal, right? We have worked in hundreds of parishes and this is not normal."

Their response was perfect: "It's normal *here*."

A LITTLE THEOLOGY OF FRUIT-BEARING

When embarking on a journey, it is extremely useful to consult a map in advance. Think of this chapter as a very brief introduction, a Catholic map of fruit-bearing.

Theology is the exploration of God's self-revelation, without which we could not know God. But what the Church calls God's "*economy*" refers "to all the works by which God reveals himself and communicates his life" to humanity in time and space (CCC 236). God's economy is about *subjective*, or *applied*, redemption — that is, how God's grace pours into our world and changes our individual lives, families, neighborhoods, parish communities, and whole cities. In the economy of God, when we walk obediently with Jesus as his disciple in the midst of his Church, you and I gradually become God's "handiwork, created in Christ Jesus for the good works that God has prepared" (Ephesians 2:10) and through which he reveals himself and communicates his life to the world. *We become fruit.*

In John 15, "fruit" (Greek: *karpos*) as a metaphor refers to a "deed, action, result, profit, or gain."[1] In other words, it is something real and concrete that most ordinary people can recognize as good or bad. The word "fruit" in Catholic Tradition is used to refer to a spectrum of related but different things:

1. The interior spiritual consolations that a person may experience as he or she follows Jesus as a disciple.

2. Fruits of the Spirit. Catholic Tradition follows the Vulgate (St. Jerome's Latin translation of the Bible) in listing twelve fruits: attributes or characteristics of the Christian life: charity, joy, peace, patience,

---

[1] 2590 Karpos, *Strong's Concordance* (online at http://biblehub.com/greek/2590.htm, as of May 5, 2017).

kindness, goodness, generosity, gentleness, faithfulness, modesty, self-control, chastity.[2]
3. All personal internal and external acts of obedience and cooperation with grace.
4. What God accomplishes or offers others *through* our acts of obedience (the fruit of our fruit, so to speak).

(It is important to note that the impact of God's provision made available to others through our acts of obedience depends *also* upon the spiritual openness of the one receiving it and *that person's* response. The recipient has to choose to cooperate with the grace received through your obedience.

So, for instance, if a Christian author obeys the Holy Spirit's prompting and writes a book urging people to help the homeless, that book is a fruit of her obedience. But, for her obedience through that book to *fully* bear fruit, somebody else has to read it and respond to the call of the Holy Spirit by actually taking action to help the homeless. The fruit of another's response to the graces channeled through our "yes" can affect many lives. The fruit of the fruit of our fruit cascades out and touches many, including people we will never know.)

5. The person that you and I become through this lifelong process of cooperating with God's love and grace is also fruit; the "everlasting splendor" that C. S. Lewis spoke of in *The Weight of Glory*.[3]

The accumulated impact of our acts of obedience is largely unknowable by us in this lifetime. Any apparent fruit that is

---

[2] See *Catechism of the Catholic Church* (CCC), 1832.
[3] Lewis, *The Weight of Glory*, p. 29.

visible to us or to others is only a small glimpse of the infinitely larger network of grace that encompasses all of time and space and is known only to God. We will begin to understand the mystery of grace only when we stand before him.

I got a glimpse of the "fruit of the fruit of my fruit" a few years ago, when I received a letter from a woman I had never met. "Emily" wrote that she had driven hundreds of miles to attend a Called & Gifted workshop put on by a small team in another state. As a result of the workshop, she said that she was in the midst of missionary training and would soon be sent to Africa to train medical personnel to receive and distribute AIDS medication. Emily turned out to be a recently retired pharmacist with an epidemiology background who had not known what to do next. She had never imagined becoming a medical missionary — until she went through the gifts-discernment process and realized that she might have been given a charism of Missionary. Emily wrote to thank me for the discernment process that changed the course of her life.

I was especially moved when I considered what God might do through her obedience. Emily's part in making AIDS medication available throughout a small African country could save the lives of an entire generation and change the course of the whole nation. A few days later, I attended a parish gathering during which I had the chance to share Emily's story. A woman across the table from me became very excited. She exclaimed, "Emily's like Esther in the Bible! Who knows but that she was brought into the world for such a time as this?"

Of course! But aren't we all?

THE VINE AND THE BRANCHES

Scripture describes the Church as both the Father's cultivated field and as the vineyard in which Jesus is the "True Vine."

The Holy Spirit is the sap that runs between the Vine and branches.

In our Tradition, the imagery of fruit-bearing is used of both the Church and the Gospel. The Church is called the "Vine" because she is the mystical Body of Christ who shares in the life of her Head,[4] while St. Paul writes of the Gospel "bearing fruit and growing" (Colossians 1:6). The life-changing power of Jesus the True Vine is communicated through his Great Story to those who are not yet disciples and to those who are. Speaking the name of Jesus has great spiritual power:

> But the one name that contains everything is the one that the Son of God received in his incarnation: JESUS…. The name "Jesus" contains all: God and man and the whole economy of creation and salvation. To pray "Jesus" is to invoke him and to call him within us. His name is the only one that contains the presence it signifies. Jesus is the Risen One, and whoever invokes the name of Jesus is welcoming the Son of God who loved him and who gave himself up for him. (CCC 2666)

Jesus' name actually contains his presence and whoever invokes Jesus' name is welcoming him. Which is why naming Jesus with love and telling his story bears fruit. (And why it is sinful to take Jesus' name in vain.)

---

4 See Pope St. John Paul II, *Christifideles Laici* (on the vocation and mission of the laity), 16 (online at http://w2.vatican.va/content/john-paul-ii/en/apost_exhortations/documents/hf_jp-ii_exh_30121988_christifideles-laici.html, as of May 5, 2017).

The Vine and the Graft

You and I are not *natural* branches of the Vine. Rather, we are foreign branches *grafted* onto the Vine (see CCC 1988). What is fascinating about this image is that, in nature, the branch grafted on — *not* the rootstock vine — determines if and what quality of fruit is borne.

For instance, if I plant a white rose — perhaps a Pope John Paul II hybrid tea rose, which, by the way, has a gorgeous aroma — that has been grafted onto the rootstock of a red rose (as is true of most American roses), it will bear only white roses. But if my beautiful JPII graft on the upper part of the rose is killed by a Colorado blizzard, I will never see another white rose. The surviving root stock buried in the earth will be doing all the fruit-bearing from now on, and it is going to be red!

But in the Kingdom, it doesn't work that way. In John 15, *the Vine changes the spiritual DNA of the graft* so that the naturally fruitless graft can bear fruit. In the heavenly Vineyard, the branch does *not* determine the quality of the fruit, the Vine does. *Bearing good fruit is the evidence that the nature of the grafted branch has been fundamentally transformed by its union with the Vine.* In short, we only bear fruit if we are transformed by our union with Christ. We only bear fruit if we are living as disciples.

The Wild Olive and Root of Israel

Another powerful image from Scripture is that of Gentile Christians being "wild olive" branches grafted on to the root stock of Israel in baptism (see Romans 11:13-24). The fruit of the olive tree was precious in the ancient Mediterranean because olives were the single most important food item, used not only for cooking and healing but also as a cosmetic, as soap, and as the most important source of light.

In the ancient world, branches of cultivated, fruit-bearing olive trees were often grafted onto a rootstock of "wild" olive. The wild olive root would never bear edible fruit itself but would supply the "good," cultivated branches with nutrients so *they* could bear fruit. No ancient Greek farmer would graft a wild, non-fruit-bearing branch onto cultivated rootstock because no edible olives would be produced!

But once again, the impossible is possible in the Kingdom. We wild, unproductive Gentile branches do not bring fruitfulness to the tree of Israel. Rather, the tree makes our unfruitful branches fruitful by transforming them with God's life-giving supernatural power. *Our spiritual "DNA" is altered by being grafted into the life of Jesus Christ, the Messiah of Israel.*

> By this power of the Spirit, God's children *can bear much fruit.* He who has grafted us onto the true vine will make us bear "the fruit of the Spirit: ... love, joy, peace, patience, kindness, goodness, faithfulness, gentleness, self-control." "We live by the Spirit"; the more we renounce ourselves, the more we "walk by the Spirit." (CCC 736, emphasis added)

If we remain "in Jesus" and Jesus in us — if that graft is being transformed by the DNA of the Vine — we will bear much fruit.

What Fruit Looks Like

There is a whole set of spiritual corollaries that go with this process of transformation through union with the Vine. *If* we remain in Jesus and his word and Jesus remains in us, then:

- We bear much fruit, fruit that will remain.
- We show that we are disciples.
- We keep his commandments.
- We remain in his love.
- It brings the Father glory.
- Jesus' joy will be in us.
- Our joy will be complete.
- Our prayers will be answered (see John 15:1-16).

That sounds like a great deal to me. In meditating on this passage, I was especially struck by verse sixteen, which linked bearing fruit to having our prayers answered. Obviously, prayer itself is enormously powerful and can change the course of history. John Wesley famously said that "God does nothing except in answer to believing prayer."[5] But I am also sure that one of the reasons that our prayers will be answered is that the fruit *you* bear will turn out to be the answer to *someone else's* prayers!

FAITH AND FRUIT

The root stock of the Vine and the cultivated olive are full of the life and sap of the Holy Spirit. And that life and sap is truly and reliably given to us by the means Jesus bestowed on the Church: the gift of the indwelling Holy Spirit given to the baptized, the sacraments, the liturgy, the Scriptures, and many other gifts he has given us in and through his Body. That is why the *Catechism* says of the liturgy:

---

[5] Carey Lodge, "John Wesley: 10 Quotes on Faith, Evangelism, and Putting God First," *Christian Today*, June 28, 2016 (online at http://www.christiantoday.com/article/john.wesley.10.quotes.on.faith.evangelism.and.putting.god.first/89402.htm, as of May 5, 2017).

A sacramental celebration is a meeting of God's children with their Father, in Christ and the Holy Spirit; this meeting takes the form of a dialogue, through actions and words. Admittedly, the symbolic actions are already a language, *but the Word of God and the response of faith have to accompany and give life to them, so that the seed of the Kingdom can bear its fruit in good soil.* (CCC 1153, emphasis added)

Our spiritual openness and eagerness to enter into the obedience of faith is essential. Evangelization, personal faith, and conversion that leads to the lifelong journey of intentional discipleship changes our interior disposition, cultivates our spiritual soil, and makes it rich enough to bear much fruit.

How important is fruit-bearing to the drama of redemption? I was amazed to realize that St. Paul described it as one of the central purposes of Jesus' resurrection from the dead:

In the same way, my brothers, you also were put to death to the law through the body of Christ so that you might belong to another, *to the one who was raised from the dead in order that we might bear fruit for God.* (Romans 7:4, emphasis added)

Fruit-bearing is the primary indicator that everything that Christ accomplished for us is actually reaching us, penetrating, and changing us. Bearing fruit is the sign that salvation has come to our house and is actually occurring in our lives.

No wonder Pope St. John Paul II said:

Bearing fruit is an essential demand of life in Christ and life in the Church. The person who does not bear fruit does not remain in communion: "Each branch of mine that bears no fruit, he (my Father) takes away" (Jn 15:2).[6]

That is also why he reminded us:

> People are approached in liberty by God who calls everyone to grow, develop and bear fruit. A person cannot put off a response nor cast off personal responsibility in the matter. The solemn words of Jesus refer to this exalted and serious responsibility: "If a man does not abide in me, he is cast forth as a branch and withers; and the branches are gathered, thrown into the fire and burned" (Jn 15:6).[7]

OBSTACLES TO FRUIT-BEARING

Dogmatic theologian Ludwig Ott summed up the interior dynamic of fruit-bearing this way: "the subjective disposition of the recipient is … the indispensable pre-condition of the communication of grace."[8]

Infants cannot put obstacles in the way of receiving grace, but older children, teens, and adults certainly can. The obstacles that can block the ultimate fruitfulness of valid sacraments include:

- Lack of personal faith.
- Lack of understanding.
- Lack of a desire to live a new life.
- Lack of repentance.

---

[6] Pope St. John Paul II, *Christifideles Laici*, 32.
[7] Ibid., 57.
[8] Ludwig Ott, *Fundamentals of Catholic Dogma* (Charlotte, NC: TAN Books, 2009), p. 330.

In his classic book, *A Key to the Doctrine of the Eucharist*, Abbot Vonier uses a powerful image to convey how obstacles can block the living impact of graces that we have objectively received:

> [It is] a favorite idea of St. Thomas, that faith is truly a contact with Christ.... Without this contact of faith, we are dead unto Christ, the stream of his life passes us by without entering into us, as a rock in the midst of a river remains unaffected by the turbulent rush of waters.... Till the contact of faith be established, the great redemption has not become *our* redemption; the things of Christ are not ours in any true sense.[9]

CATHOLIC IDENTITY AND FRUITFULNESS

It is important that we understand that what is sometimes called "Catholic identity" is not necessarily an expression of living faith or discipleship. In an ideal world, personal faith and discipleship *would* always form the center of one's Catholic identity. But in our generation, many Western people who still hold on to the name "Catholic" are functional agnostics or atheists — even if they occasionally drop by a parish. Catholic identity *alone* will not produce genuine fruit. Jews who presumed their spiritual status was assured because they were born to Jewish parents were schooled by John the Baptist in no uncertain terms — terms that apply just as much to us:

> "Produce good fruits as evidence of your repentance; and do not begin to say to yourselves, 'We have Abraham as

---

9 Dom Anscar Vonier, *A Key to the Doctrine of the Eucharist* (Assumption Press, 2013), p. 3, emphasis added.

our father,' for I tell you, God can raise up children to Abraham from these stones. Even now the ax lies at the root of the trees. Therefore every tree that does not produce good fruit will be cut down and thrown into the fire." (Luke 3:8-9)

Being active in your parish is not a guarantee either. You and I can be very active in our parish as catechists, musicians, members of the RCIA team, or the finance council. We can run capital campaigns, serve as ushers, and help with parish festivals. But all that activity is not necessarily fruit just because it takes place in a religious setting.

Fruit-bearing always emerges out of a growing relationship with God. Bearing spiritual fruit occurs when we act *because* we are seeking, however haltingly, to say "yes" to God's love, grace, inspiration, or command. It can be difficult for devoted Catholics to believe that there are people who do not serve in church settings out of a personal faith. I was stunned when I first met active Catholics who told me they had no relationship with God.

For instance, I once attended an invitation-only national evangelization conference where a middle-aged man I didn't know walked up to me at the first break. He startled me when he said "Until I read your book last month, I did not know it was possible to have a personal relationship with God." That was *not* the sort of thing I expected to hear in a gathering like that!

This man was obviously a good guy and a highly committed Catholic. In fact, he was in full-time ministry forming clergy. So I asked him to help me understand why he thought he had not known that he could have a relationship with God. He said he was raised in a faithful, practicing Catholic family, but no one had ever talked about a relationship with God. He just had not known it was possible.

Since *Forming Intentional Disciples* was published, I have had similar conversations all over the world with bishops, seminary faculty, priests, religious, and lay leaders. They told me that when they were ordained or took final vows or began ministry, they had not been intentional disciples ... but they were *now*. The fun part was hearing the amazing stories of encounter and how following Jesus had transformed their lives and ministries.

In every parish that is beginning to evangelize, the issue of leaders who are not yet disciples naturally emerges — as it should. One friend who is in parish ministry told me that staff members are coming to him acknowledging, "I am not a disciple yet." What he reported and I have also witnessed is that most Catholics who come to this awareness don't feel judged or a failure. They are just becoming aware of new spiritual possibilities. They are interested, open, and hungry, but they don't know what to do.

When this happens, here are some suggestions that my friend and I have found useful:

1. Leave the conversation open-ended so that you can return to it. Offer to meet again if possible.
2. Pray right there and then if the individual is comfortable. I find that helping people to pray out loud and to acknowledge to God that they are open to spiritual and personal change and ready for more is very powerful. You are helping someone cross into the threshold of openness, a transition that can be very difficult.[10] In my experience, God always answers that prayer in a powerful way.

---

[10] For more on the threshold of openness, read pp. 155-166 in *Forming Intentional Disciples.*

3. If a solid trust exists between the two of you, and you have the time and privacy, consider having a threshold conversation. Threshold conversations are very simple, open-ended spiritual conversations — a kind of listening evangelization that helps you get a sense of where people have been in their spiritual journey and where they are now. You can have a meaningful threshold conversation in ten minutes — or much longer, depending upon what your friend has to say! A simple way to broach the topic is to say that if your friend feels comfortable, you would love to hear the story of his or her lived relationship or experience of God to this point in life. If people are willing to tell you their story, your job is to listen intently to understand what that journey has been like from their perspective.[11] We have seen people move through whole thresholds just by telling their story to someone who really listened.

4. Look for individuals to whom the seeker is close and who are spiritually farther along and help those friends reach out to support this individual as he or she grows closer to Jesus.

5. Is this individual already involved with or attending existing evangelization experiences, retreats, courses, or other opportunities at the parish or local level? If so, ask how those experiences are affecting him or her. If your friend is not yet involved, help him or her get connected.

---

[11] For more about how to have a threshold conversation, read pp. 191-199 in *Forming Intentional Disciples.*

A WORLD IN SPIRITUAL MOTION

I find it enormously helpful to keep reminding myself that everyone I meet is in spiritual motion. A man could essentially sleepwalk through his baptism because he fell in love with a Catholic girl and was jumping through the hoops of the RCIA process just to please his future in-laws. Then ten years later, he can experience a massive conversion and awaken to the power of the Gospel in amazing ways. Meanwhile, one of his friends might go through a period of spiritual fervor in high school and then lose interest while in college and walk away from both Jesus and his Catholic identity. Both possibilities (and many, many others) are present throughout our lives. St. Thomas Aquinas describes it this way: One can seek intentionally to grow in grace *after* baptism while another, through post-baptismal negligence, "*baffles* grace."[12]

It seems incredible that puny human beings can baffle the grace of God by our lack of cooperation, but it is true. And to the extent that we do, we will bear little or no fruit. A classic observation by St. Francis de Sales is an essential corrective if we are going to live the lifelong conversion known as discipleship:

> I am glad that you make a daily new beginning; there is no better means of progress in the spiritual life than to be continually beginning afresh.[13]

---

[12] St. Thomas Aquinas, *Summa Theologiae*, III, q69, a8 (online at http://www.newadvent.org/summa/4069.htm#article8, as of May 5, 2017).

[13] St. Francis de Sales, "To a Lady. On the Distractions of a Busy Life. May 19, 1609," in *A Selection from the Spiritual Letters of St. Francis de Sales*, translated by H. L. Sidney Lear (New York: E. P. Dutton and Company, 1876), p. 122.

LACK OF PRAYER IS AN OBSTACLE

One very significant obstacle to fruit-bearing is lack of prayer, which is at the heart of a relationship with God. Without prayer, all of our activity risks being fruitless. Recall that the seed in the parable dies not only when the birds eat it or when it falls on barren soil, but when it is choked by thorns that are "worldly anxiety, the lure of riches, and the craving for other things" (Mark 4:19).

That is why Pope Francis urges:

> Let us call upon him today, firmly rooted in prayer, for without prayer all our activity risks being fruitless and our message empty. Jesus wants evangelizers who proclaim the good news not only with words but above all by a life transfigured by God's presence.[14]

DISCIPLE-MAKERS AS FRUIT-FARMERS

The *Catechism* tells us:

> The fruit of sacramental life is both personal and ecclesial. For every one of the faithful on the one hand, this fruit is life for God in Christ Jesus; for the Church, on the other, it is an increase in charity and in her mission of witness. (CCC 1134)

For every one of us, the fruit we bear has a profound impact on our personal maturation and holiness as disciples in Christ. But your fruit also increases the evangelical capacity of the

---

[14] Pope Francis, *Evangelii Gaudium*, 259.

whole Church: her love and ability to bear witness to Christ. The mission and compassion of the whole Church is *fueled* by your fruit. Today's "nones" and "former Catholics" are seldom interested in our insider debates but are really intrigued and moved by the fruit that Christians bear. The fruit we bear "reveals" the presence and the love of God. Our fruit builds powerful bridges of spiritual trust and rouses spiritual curiosity. In the communion of saints, your fruit belongs to and somehow touches every other baptized person. But it is also true that the fruit that we were anointed by the Holy Spirit to bear but do *not* bear is a profound loss to both the Church and the world. In the economy of God, your fruit, my fruit, and the fruit borne by the whole Church is both a form of prayer and an answer to the world's prayers.

There is someone out there right now who is waiting for what you have been given to give, and their life, their spiritual and personal destiny, hangs in the balance. You may not have met them yet. They may not even have been born yet, but in God's providence, *you are the one.* It *matters* that you say "yes."

So, what does this mean for those of us serving in some form of pastoral leadership? What does it mean to lead, to pastor, to govern a community of missionary disciples and fruit-bearers? Pope St. John Paul II describes it this way:

> This *munus regendi* [governance] represents a very delicate and complex duty which, in addition to the attention which must be given to a variety of persons and their vocations, also involves the ability to coordinate all the gifts and charisms which the Spirit inspires in the community, to discern them and to put them to good use for the upbuilding of the Church in constant union with the bishops.[15]

---

[15] Pope St. John Paul II, *Pastores Dabo Vobis*, 26.

All Catholic leaders — ordained or not — are, in a real way, called to be *fruit-farmers*, not just spiritual seed-scatterers. Everything we do is for the sake of producing an abundant harvest. Sustained, intentional evangelization changes everything by enriching the spiritual soil of individuals, families, and whole parish communities. Making disciples creates the conditions that will enable our sacramental seeds, which are filled with the life of God, to germinate, grow, and bear a rich harvest of fruit that will nourish the Church and bring Christ to the world.

CHAPTER 3

The Undaunted Fruit-Farmer

He changed the desert into pools of water,
arid land into springs of water,
And settled the hungry there;
they built a city to live in.
They sowed fields and planted vineyards,
brought in an abundant harvest.

PSALM 107:35-37

Years ago, I moved from Seattle — locals call it "Rain City" — to Colorado Springs, 6,700 feet high in the Rockies and semi-arid. I bought a "fixer-upper" home filled with tons of potential and not much else. My first clue about how bad things had been was when total strangers thanked me the first time I mowed the dead stubble that passed for a lawn, saying, "Nobody has done that in years!" I watered for a year, but nothing grew except three-foot-high Canadian thistles.

Finally, I brought in a very savvy landscape designer. She took one look and summed up my yard with brisk precision: "There's nothing here to save." She was not saying "Abandon all hope, you can't have a garden in Colorado." She meant, "You are going to have to start from scratch. You can't garden in Colorado the way you gardened in Seattle where rain regularly falls from the sky." When I asked her how long it would take for a new garden to reach maturity, she calculated for a moment. "Eight years."

So, I double-dug flower beds, hauled in good soil, planted, fertilized, and watered. I pruned and mulched, and replanted when things failed. I bribed male relatives, friends, and seminarians to tackle some of the toughest tasks and hired skilled help when I needed it. I beat off marauding deer and rabbits. Together, the garden and I survived blizzards and hail bombs. I would stalk around the garden on cool summer mornings, trowel in hand, rejoicing in the color and light. Eight years, fourteen water-wise trees, sixty-five hardy shrubs, and hundreds of tough-as-nails perennials later, I found out that my landscape designer was right. A lush, green, and undaunted garden with a view of Pikes Peak now completely fills what was once the neighborhood eyesore.

I have often used the story of my garden to illustrate the dramatic cultural shifts we have lived through over the past fifty years. Our "spiritual climate" has also changed dramatically, and so has the life of the Church. Our culture is now an arid spiritual place, a far more hostile and difficult place to make disciples and foster apostles. But that does not mean we cannot evangelize and bear abundant fruit in the twenty-first century. It just means we cannot do it the way we once did when the culture generally supported our faith and values.

Baptized Unbelievers

Pope Emeritus Benedict XVI demonstrated his awareness of our quickly changing situation when he significantly rewrote the conclusion to an essay on the indissolubility of marriage he first published in 1972 and then republished in 2014. The pope did not mince words:

Today there is another question that imposes itself with great seriousness. Currently there are more and more baptized pagans, meaning persons who have become Christian by means of baptism but do not believe and have never known the faith. This is a paradoxical situation: baptism makes the person Christian, but without faith he remains nonetheless just a baptized pagan.... This brings up questions for which we still do not have answers. And therefore it is even more urgent to explore them.[1]

This reality, which the Vatican has also referred to as "baptized unbelievers," is something all evangelizers must grapple with. Right now, many children who are being baptized have parents who neither believe nor practice the faith and are not attempting to pass the faith on to their children. A recent CARA study found that only 14 percent of millennial Catholics — who are in their peak child-bearing years — attend Mass on a weekly basis,[2] so it isn't startling to find that only 11 percent of millennial Catholic parents have enrolled their children in some kind of parish-based religious education.[3] Sixty-eight

---

[1] J. Ratzinger-Benedikt XVI, "Einführung in das Christentum. Bekenntnis, Taufe, Nachfolge," Joseph Ratzinger Gesammelte Schriften, Band 4, Verlag Herder, Freiburg, 2014. For more information, see Sandro Magister, "In the Synod on the Family Even the Pope Emeritus Is Speaking Out," *Chiesa*, December 3, 2014 (online at http://chiesa.espresso.repubblica.it /articolo/1350933bdc4.html?eng=y, as of May 5, 2017).

[2] Mark M. Grey, "Sacraments Today Updated," *Nineteen Sixty-Four* blog, Center for Applied Research in the Apostolate, August 16, 2016 (online at http://nineteensixty-four.blogspot.com/2016/08/sacraments-today-updated .html, as of May 5, 2017).

[3] Center for Applied Research in the Apostolate, *Practice of Faith in the Catholic Family*, August 2015, p. 6.

percent of *all* Catholic parents have not enrolled their children in any type of formal religious education.[4]

We need all hands on deck because we are standing on the edge of a demographic precipice. In Britain, it is even grimmer. There, 65 percent of Catholics are either marginal or non-practicing or on their way out the door. Nearly half of non-practicing British Catholics are functioning agnostics or believers in an impersonal God, and more than half of Catholics who leave were already *de facto* agnostics or atheists.[5] The irony is that UK "leavers" have *not* left the practice of "their" faith. *They are practicing their faith when they leave the Church because their actual faith is closer to agnosticism than Catholicism.*

No matter where we live in the Western world, it is critical to remember that when we encounter a non-practicing Catholic or a "none," we are probably not speaking to someone who just likes to sleep in on Sundays. There is a good chance that we are talking to someone whose belief in a personal God is tenuous or nonexistent.

Institute trainers have been working intensely with many parishes and dioceses, helping them begin calling parishioners to intentional, fruit-bearing discipleship, and we have learned a great deal over the past five years. Here are some of our most significant recent "ahas."

1. Beware of "Imagined" Evangelization

When there is such a gap between the worldview and experience of so many unbelievers and the beliefs and experience of

---

4   Dr. Gregory K. Popcak, "A crisis among Catholic families," *OSV Newsweekly*, July 1, 2015 (online at https://www.osv.com/OSVNewsweekly/ByIssue /Article/TabId/735/ArtMID/13636/ArticleID/17797/A-crisis-among -Catholic-families.aspx, as of May 5, 2017).

5   Stephen Bullivant, "Catholic Disaffiliation in Britain: A Quantitative Overview," *Journal of Contemporary Religion*, 2016, Vol. 31, No. 2, pp. 189-192.

ecclesial insiders, it is fatally easy to underestimate how far *we, the evangelizers*, will have to travel in order to bring the Gospel to the majority of people. Recently, blogger Colleen Vermeulen remarked on an observation Pope Francis made:

> Pope Francis has reminded those who preach Eucharistic homilies to "never respond to questions that nobody asks" when it comes to sharing the Gospel (*Evangelii Gaudium*, para. 155). Let us follow a similar path, avoiding *imagined evangelization*, where we lead with answers the unchurched have no interest in; and instead, taking up a *people-driven evangelization* that brings us alongside those who are not at our Eucharistic Table, yet have a desire for and interest in closeness to God.[6]

That's why the new *Pew Religious Landscape Survey* below is so fascinating and important. It shows us a hidden field that is full of unexpected, wild wheat.

2. We Are Everywhere

In 2014, the new *Pew Religious Landscape Survey*[7] found that 45 percent of U.S. adults (approximately 110 million) are "connected" in some important way to Catholicism. This means that 110 million Americans feel some important bond with the Catholic Church or the Catholic faith. No other religious

---

[6] Colleen Vermeulen, "Imagined Evangelization vs. People-Driven Evangelization," *New Evangelizers* blog, May 30, 2016 (online at http://newevangelizers.com/blog/2016/05/30/imagined-evangelization-vs-people-driven-evangelization/, as of May 5, 2017).

[7] Pew Research Center, "U.S. Catholics Open to Non-Traditional Families," September 2, 2015 (online at http://www.pewforum.org/2015/09/02/u-s-catholics-open-to-non-traditional-families/, as of May 5, 2017).

tradition in the United States has anything like this reach. *It means that nearly one out of every two American adults you meet has some kind of significant tie to the Church.*

There are four basic categories of Catholic connections.

First: Twenty percent of U.S. adults have a Catholic identity. Ask them their religion and roughly 49 million American adults will say, "I'm Catholic." Of these Catholics, 22 percent attend Mass weekly, but the majority seldom or never cross the threshold.[8] But that still leaves 61 million other people who also feel a significant connection to the faith in some way or other, yet who do not self-identify as Catholic. Who are they?

Second: This is where the real surprise comes in. The second cohort of people with a significant connection to the Church are the *9 percent of American adults (22 million) who say they are not Catholic religiously but who nonetheless feel "culturally" or "partially" Catholic anyway.* Half of these "partial" Catholics currently describe themselves as Protestant and half as "nones" (people who do not belong to any particular religious group) or as belonging to some other faith. The majority, 65 percent of this group, were raised Catholic and left both the Church and the identity but *still* feel connected in significant ways. And 43 percent of these "cultural" or "partial" Catholics stated that they are open to returning!

I was particularly startled to learn that one-third of these cultural Catholics were not raised Catholic and didn't have Catholic parents but *still* consider themselves to be Catholic in some meaningful way. We don't even have a category for the millions of people who have no Catholic background at all but nevertheless identify as at least partly Catholic. They need the intentional accompaniment of Catholic disciples to help them encounter Jesus Christ within the Church.

---

[8] Grey, "Sacraments Today Updated."

Third: Another 9 percent of American adults — that is, another 22 million people — call themselves "ex-Catholics." These are not merely people who drifted away from the faith but are rather people who *define* themselves as having left the Church. It is a harder stance, often fueled by some kind of wound or anger or disbelief. Yet even among that group, 8 percent (1.7 million) told Pew that they were open to returning. In our Making Disciples seminars, we have a motto, "Never accept a label in place of a story," because even an "ex-Catholic" might be open to coming back.

Fourth: This final group — which includes 8 percent of American adults (20 million people) — feel "connected" to Catholicism through Catholic family, friends, institutions, practices, or values.

Remember that this is a snapshot in time. All of these numbers might be significantly different in a few years because religious identity in the twenty-first century west is highly fluid. Many people who now define themselves as ex-Catholics may change their minds (with our help), while many who now identify as Catholic may soon identify as ex-Catholic.

We stand at a stunning crossroads: millions are jettisoning their Catholic identity but simultaneously nearly half the adult population of the United States feels some serious connection to the Catholic Church. Every one of those connections is a potential bridge of trust across which we can walk as evangelizers to invite them to begin the journey to intentional discipleship, either by way of return (for former Catholics) or baptism. What an incredible evangelical opportunity if we have the will to take advantage of it!

3. To Be Deep in Catholic History Is to Evangelize

No, Virginia. Evangelization is *not* Protestant. Few Catholics seem to remember an influential pre-Vatican II evangelization movement that was driven by two things: the rapid secularization of Europe and the experience of missionaries outside "Christendom." I had never heard of the kerygmatic movement until I read Father Alfonso Nebreda, S.J.'s out-of-print classic, *Kerygma in Crisis?* Father Nebreda showed that Catholic catechesis had clearly taught the critical importance of personal faith in centuries past:

> Early sixteenth-century catechisms routinely empha-sized personal faith in the work of Jesus Christ as essen-tial to salvation. ... The sixteenth-century catechisms placed faith at the beginning of the baptismal act. We read, for instance, in the catechism of Dietenberger (1537): "Sacramental baptism demands three impor-tant things: faith, water, and the divine Word, and none of these may be lacking. Water and the word do not suffice, *the word and water are nothing without faith*.
>
> ... the Contarini catechism says, referring to St. Thomas: "Sacraments are exterior and sensible signs of the invisible grace which is bestowed through them *on account of faith in Christ's death* by which our sins are forgiven."[9]

However, by the late sixteenth century and into the first half of the twentieth century, catechisms shifted their focus almost entirely to the objective efficacy of the sacraments and hardly mentioned the personal act of faith. Why the change?

For centuries, the Church was under sustained attack by a series of challenges from (1) the Protestant Reformation, (2) the anti-clericalism of the French Revolution, and (3)

---

[9] Alfonso M. Nebreda, S.J., *Kerygma in Crisis?* (Chicago: Loyola University Press, 1965), pp. 35-36, emphasis added.

the eighteenth-century emphasis on pure reason. As a result, the Church's teaching increasingly focused on those aspects of the faith being attacked by her critics."[10] Understandably, Catholics doubled down on teaching the truth that baptism was not a mere symbol and had the power to regenerate and to incorporate the believer into the life of the Blessed Trinity. The need for personal faith in the redemptive work of Jesus Christ as a disciple was de-emphasized because it seemed too similar to the Protestant emphasis on *sola fide*, salvation by "faith *alone*." From the perspective of the average lay Catholic, being faithful came to mean assenting to true doctrines taught by the Church and obeying the laws of the Church. I personally cannot begin to count the number of older Catholics who have told me: "I was 60 or 70 before I realized that being Catholic was not just about rules but about a relationship."

Father Nebreda describes the ensuing dramatic shift in catechetical emphasis:

> Faith is no longer seen as an indispensable condition for the efficacy of the sacraments or as the basis on which the whole sacramental world and the sacramental communication of salvation rests. In contrast, tradition has fondly called them *sacramenta fidei* ["sacraments of faith"], attributing their power to the *fides passionis* ["faith in the passion"].[11]

By the beginning of the twentieth century, de-Christianization was already very advanced in France. The circumstance sounds very much like our current situation:

> French pastors preparing children for solemn Communion realized that, unless something were done, these

---

[10] Ibid., pp. 3-4, 8, 30-31, 37.
[11] Ibid., p. 36..

children would return to a home where no one believed. Moreover, the home situation was such that it might even prevent the child from continuing to live his faith. In such a situation, the old-type catechesis seemed terribly inadequate.[12]

A new emphasis on personal faith and discipleship emerged among Catholic missionary leaders in the 1930s. By the late 1950s, "international study weeks" brought together hundreds of missionaries and catechetical leaders to discuss these burning issues. The meeting in 1960 was when kerygmatic leaders first articulated their basic principle:

> The aim of the catechetical apostolate is not knowledge as such but living faith — man's response to God.[13]

The whole concept of "pre-evangelization" (now incorporated into formal Church teaching as one of the three essential stages of pre-baptismal evangelization: pre-evangelization, initial proclamation, initiatory catechesis[14]) was first clearly articulated at the 1962 study week in Bangkok, Thailand.

4. Pre-Evangelization Is Key in the Twenty-First-Century West

Father Nebreda was a Spanish missionary to Japan. He knew that among the Japanese, there was commonly no concept of God at all. Father Nebreda emphasized the need for pre-evangelization to prepare people in this setting to hear and respond to the kerygma, the story of what Jesus has accomplished for us. We

---

[12] Ibid., p. 41.
[13] Ibid., p. 39.
[14] *National Directory for Catechesis* (Washington: USCCB, 2005), pp. 49-50.

must begin much further back in order to meet people with this worldview where they are and to bring them to a place where the story of what Jesus has accomplished on their behalf begins to make sense.

"This work of first conditioning the human ground before sowing the divine seed [pre-evangelization] has always been done by the best missionaries and pastors."[15] Here the value of understanding the thresholds of conversion becomes even more apparent.

For the millions who no longer believe or trust the Church or Christians, some kind of bridge of *trust* must be built or else they cannot move closer. That trust must be intentionally strengthened over time until spiritual *curiosity* awakens: curiosity, in particular, about the person and work of Jesus Christ. And that curiosity needs to be fostered and grow more intense until a person is willing to become *open* to the possibility of the kind of change that a relationship with Jesus introduces into our lives. Pre-evangelization helps people make the journey through the first three thresholds, from distrust to early openness.

Father Nebreda shares a very moving experience at the end of his book. He had spoken about the meaning of life and death at a Japanese Catholic university. The next day, a young woman student called to make an appointment with him. She claimed to be an atheist. Her first stunning question was "Why can't I kill my father?" Her father had been incurably ill for fifteen years and had recently asked his wife and daughter to hasten his death.

For over an hour, Father Nebreda listened deeply and prayerfully, seeking to understand her real concerns. Finally, she invited his response: "What do *you* really think?" He replied:

"You see, for me everything is different. ... I also have my own sorrows and difficulties; I am in anguish too,

---

[15] Nebreda, *Kerygma in Crisis?*, p. 66.

by many things I do not understand. But for me, it is different because I believe firmly that behind everything is the hand of God and behind the hand of God is always the heart of God." [16]

As a result of that conversation, the student began to think seriously about "the mystery of God who is a Father, who has a heart." Not only did she *not* kill her father, but she was eventually baptized as a Catholic. [17]

In a post-modern setting where non-practicing Catholics are flooding out of the Church and children are increasingly raised without any faith, our first response often needs to be pre-evangelization, not catechesis. As the U.S. bishops explain:

> First, the listeners are prepared for the first proclamation of the Gospel, or *pre-evangelization*. Pre-evangelization ordinarily builds on basic human needs, such as security, love, or acceptance, and shows how those basic human needs include a desire for God and his word. [18]

Part of the work of pre-evangelization involves not only clearing away intellectual obstacles to faith but also helping people get in touch with their own desire for more from life: for goodness, hope, love, truth, beauty, and a meaning and purpose to life that can't be taken away. We need to recognize that in our generation, pre-evangelization is essential and often the first task of "faith formation."

The *Catechism* describes abundant fruit-bearing and exercising the charisms as a form of pre-evangelization:

---

[16] Ibid., pp. 128-134.
[17] Ibid.
[18] *National Directory for Catechesis*, p. 49, emphasis in original.

"... God willed that external proofs of his Revelation should be joined to the internal helps of the Holy Spirit." Thus the miracles of Christ and the saints, prophecies, the Church's growth and holiness, and her fruitfulness and stability "are the most certain signs of divine Revelation, adapted to the intelligence of all"; they are "motives of credibility" (*motiva credibilitatis*), which show that the assent of faith is "by no means a blind impulse of the mind." (CCC 156)

The Church adds that we have an obligation to manifest what Scripture calls the "new man" and thereby reveal the power of the Holy Spirit:

"All Christians by the example of their lives and the witness of their word, wherever they live, have an obligation to manifest the new man which they have put on in Baptism and to reveal the power of the Holy Spirit by whom they were strengthened at Confirmation." (CCC 2472, quoting *Ad Gentes*, 11)

Direct pre-evangelization of individuals includes praying for others, building genuine friendships, fostering personal and spiritual trust, hospitality, the witness of your life and vocation, having threshold and spiritual conversations with individuals, asking thought-provoking questions to stimulate spiritual curiosity, and sharing the story of what you have seen God do in your own life. It also includes the exercise of the charisms God has given you and living the vocation(s) to which God has called you.

5. Pre-Evangelization of Cultures and Structures

The Church's task of evangelization also includes a type of pre-evangelization directed to the transformation of human structures and cultures:

"Direct pre-evangelization" seeks to prepare, to set the stage for *individuals* to encounter Christ. "Indirect or collective" pre-evangelization attends to the structures and mentality of the milieu which influences the individual. Social, cultural, and economic realities can close people off to the faith. *"Indirect pre-evangelization" changes and enriches the social, cultural, and economic "soil" so it now supports the full humanity and the spiritual growth of individuals and families rather than close them off to the faith.*[19]

All disciple-makers need to be attuned to the necessity of *both* kinds of pre-evangelization, but "indirect pre-evangelization" — the pre-evangelization of secular human structures and cultures — is primarily the province of lay apostles.[20] The pre-evangelization of cultures includes praying for the spiritual renewal of one's city, neighborhood, or workplace; building relationships and spiritual trust; integrating your faith with your work and relationships, striving for apostolic excellence in one's profession or work; serving the poor and suffering; advocating for justice; leading or participating in initiatives that serve the common good, peacemaking, and so on. The exercise of your charisms and living your vocation(s) is absolutely central to the pre-evangelization of culture.

---

[19] *National Directory for Catechesis*, p. 49.

[20] See *Lumen Gentium* (Dogmatic Constitution on the Church), 36 (online at http://www.vatican.va/archive/hist_councils/ii_vatican_council/documents /vat-ii_const_19641121_lumen-gentium_en.html, as of May 5, 2017).

6. What Is My Part?

All evangelizers need to be attuned to the necessity of both kinds of pre-evangelization as well as proclamation of Jesus and catechesis, but most of us will be called, in practice, to specialize according to our individual charisms and vocations.

I've met Catholics who were totally focused on their prayer life and believed that was all that was necessary for an effective witness. Others were passionate about pre-evangelization but never moved on to explicit proclamation of the kerygma. For still others, preaching the kerygma loud and clear was obviously the key to evangelization. And many focused on catechesis because that is where they saw people encounter Jesus.

These are all non-negotiable developmental stages in calling others to conversion. *All* must take place with equal vigor in local parishes and dioceses. What can confuse us is that *individual* evangelizers can and often should focus their efforts on specific stages in the journey. My charisms and vocation may prepare me to contribute most intensely to pre-evangelization or direct proclamation or to nurturing the personal spiritual lives of those who are called and gifted to do those things. The Body of Christ, as a whole, does it all. *But individual members of that Body may be called to focus on one particular stage in the journey, while knowing that their specific personal call and gifts empower the great overall mission.*

7. There Is No Silver Bullet

Ever since *Forming Intentional Disciples* was published, we have had lots of Catholic pastors and leaders contact us, looking for the "solution" to their evangelization challenges. They are looking for the one-size-fits-all formula — the sure-fire, four-easy-step program to complete parish renewal in a year. Alas, it doesn't exist.

There is no one approach, book, devotion, organizational strategy, apostolate, or movement that can answer all our needs. There is not just one "anointed" tool or retreat or approach. There are dozens of different evangelizing approaches emerging right now that address different dimensions of our mission. We will always need to discern their roots in our Tradition and their actual fruit, but we need many tools in our evangelizing craftsman's toolbox, not just one!

My motto is "Let a thousand flowers bloom in a thousand different places." If someone else is doing a particularly great job in one part of the vineyard, don't waste your time duplicating or competing with them. We do not really need that one-hundredth minimally different kerygmatic parish retreat in English. The whole world and every human being on the planet is our mission field. Ask the Lord to direct you to a neglected area and become the apostle to that place.

8. We Need to Provide More Opportunities to Deliberately Choose Discipleship

One of the things that have become very obvious is that the average parish seldom or never offers Catholics a safe, clear opportunity to make a conscious decision to follow Jesus Christ as his disciple — to "drop one's net," as I call it in *Forming Intentional Disciples*. We presumed that the decision happened quietly and seamlessly in the course of sacramental prep and catechesis. Now we know that, for many, little or nothing happened. The penny never dropped. The culture of silence about the Gospel *must* be broken. All kinds of people, baptized or not, must be given the unpressured space to step apart from the crowd and make a meaningful, personal "yes" to follow Jesus in his Church. That includes teens and children, because children as young as four or five can make meaningful decisions to follow Jesus.

It has been very exciting to see field-tested evangelizing retreats or courses like Alpha or Discovering Christ being used in hundreds of American parishes over the past five years. I've heard the stories of thousands of Catholics whose spiritual and personal lives are being redirected and transformed as they begin following Jesus in the midst of his Church. But we need to give our people even more opportunities to grapple with the kerygma, move through the thresholds, and drop their nets — and they do not all have to be prepackaged. We hear the stories of out-of-the-box things that creative evangelizers are doing on the Forming Intentional Disciples Facebook Forum all the time.[21]

For instance, in one dynamic evangelizing parish, the youth ministry team offered a retreat for their teens that was mostly twenty-four-hour Eucharistic Adoration: open-ended encounter with Jesus. Every teen received a little fishing net (the kind you use to scoop goldfish out of an aquarium) and was explicitly challenged to wrestle with the question: Am I ready to drop my nets and follow Jesus? One woman who was present as a chaperone was watching over the Adoration chapel in the middle of the night. She said there was a teenage boy on his knees in front of the Blessed Sacrament with his fishing net. As the night wore on, he slowly edged closer to the Tabernacle on his knees. Finally, he threw his net on the ground. That parish had given that boy a safe and profound non-verbal way to say "yes" to following Jesus.

---

[21] The Forming Intentional Disciples Forum on Facebook is a very active, closed 7,000-plus-member international web community of Catholic evangelizing practitioners. The Forum hosts a 24/7 online English language discussion on *only one topic*: how to evangelize and make disciples in the twenty-first century. To join the conversation, search Facebook for the Forming Intentional Disciples Forum and click on the icon that says "I'd like to join." It helps us to know that this is the conversation for you if your personal Facebook page makes it clear that you are Catholic!

9. Making Disciples Is a Long Obedience

In the final analysis, building a fruit-bearing parish must be thought of as a *long* obedience. Like creating a Rocky Mountain garden from scratch, building a parish culture of intentional discipleship is not something that happens overnight. I recently asked one friend who has successfully led the charge in his parish how long it would take for him to do it again in another parish, now that he has a better sense of what is involved. He thought for a moment and then replied, "Six to eight years, if the parish is established, because it takes a lot longer to change the culture of an established organization. Four years if the parish is newly founded."

We've worked with a number of pastors and evangelizing leaders who have experienced maximum frustration around the three to three-and-a-half-year mark. Paradoxically, they are frustrated because they are seeing transformation. As a parish community awakens to the possibilities and evangelizers start to see genuine change, it is natural to want to see the transformation happen even faster.

In the early years, evangelizing leaders can feel isolated, as though they are fighting a resistant parish cultural norm by themselves. But then a parish community can hit that mysterious "tipping point" when the spiritual hunger of the people, not the efforts of evangelizers, becomes the driving force. People begin to take the initiative, to seek out opportunities for prayer and to talk about Jesus and their real spiritual questions. Spiritual seekers just "show up" in the parish because they heard good things were happening there. Charisms begin to manifest in surprising ways. Suddenly, evangelizing leaders find themselves running to try to keep up with the Holy Spirit and the spiritual hunger of their people. It is a very good sign.

One of the most crucial things necessary to sustain the spiritual growth of many people and the wonderful harvest of fruit-bearing is continuity of direction and leadership. We have witnessed a number of parishes that begin to see lots of lives being changed, but then everything comes to a screeching halt because a critically important leader — clergy or lay — leaves and the person who assumes leadership has no interest in evangelization. Just as both new and established gardens need attentive gardeners to foster their long-term growth and fruitfulness, so long-term, disciple-making initiatives need long-term leadership.

Parishes need many keepers of the flame, not just one, if the vision of fostering fruit-bearing discipleship is going to become normative and not centered on a single person. Ideally, the visionary leadership team would include the pastor and the most influential leaders in the parish, whether they are part of the staff or not. In some of the parishes where we have worked, the pastor is leading the charge. In others, pastors come and go, so lay leaders have sustained the direction. Transformation of the parish culture and the emergence of many intentional disciples happens where the flame burns bright long-term in the hearts of a savvy band of committed disciple-makers.

I have worked with hundreds of priests over the past few years. While I have a vivid appreciation for the institutional pressures that result in pastors moving from parish to parish on a frequent basis, I need to be very direct. The future of the Church — of our children and young adults, and of our institutions (our dioceses and parishes and schools) — is absolutely dependent upon the number of new disciples and apostles who are emerging in our midst *right now and in the future*.

All our Catholic institutions — especially our parishes, which are the only contact point that 98 percent of Catholics have with the Church — have to get truly serious about our primary mission. Both a pastor who is leaving a parish and the pastor who is coming in — no matter how different their personalities, charisms, and approaches — must share a commitment to the long-term pursuit of this most fundamental of pastoral missions. The ministerial priesthood "is directed at the *unfolding of the baptismal grace of all Christians*" (CCC 1547, emphasis added) because the salvation of billions and the future of the Church depend upon the unfolding of that grace.

Unless *all* our priests, deacons, religious, and lay leadership are grappling together with how to call every baptized person to intentional discipleship and fruit-bearing apostleship, we are headed for a demographic collapse in the next ten years that will make the post-Vatican II era look idyllic.

If, on the other hand, we seriously commit together to do what Jesus commanded us to do, we could see God do something absolutely extraordinary in our generation. There is no reason why we could not be, in our generation, like the early seventeenth-century generation of saints in France, who were the catalyst of a religious revival that changed the course of their country and the global Church.[22] But it won't happen unless we say "yes" to the long obedience of making disciples together.

---

[22] See Sherry A. Weddell, "The Generation of Saints," in *Becoming a Parish of Intentional Disciples* (Huntington, IN: Our Sunday Visitor, 2015), pp. 11-28.

CHAPTER 4

The Charismatic Is Co-Essential

*There are different kinds of spiritual gifts but the same
Spirit; there are different forms of service but the same
Lord; there are different workings but the same God who
produces all of them in everyone. To each individual the
manifestation of the Spirit is given for some benefit.*

1 CORINTHIANS 12:4-7

What could the Holy Spirit do if we say "yes" together? Let
me tell a story about the Advent I entered the Church.

The word spread like wildfire around the regional trauma
center where I was working as a temp that week. There was
an eighteen-month-old baby girl in the burn unit, dying from
third-degree burns over 90 percent of her body. She had been
immersed in scalding water from the neck down. Since no one
was clear how it had happened, Child Protective Services had
been called in, and her out-of-state family was not allowed to
have contact.

I can't explain it to this day, but I had a strong interior
sense that we didn't have to accept this, that death was not
God's will for this little girl, and that we could pray with real
confidence for her healing. I told my friend Mark about her,
and we began to pray and to ask other people to pray. Because
we were both coming into full communion with the Church

that weekend, and so living on the cusp between the Protestant and Catholic worlds, we soon had hundreds of people praying for her. Something about "Anna's" story moved everyone.

Because of my job, I was the only one who had access to Anna, so every day I would enter her room for a brief visit. I was intimidated by the nurse always at her side, so I didn't have the nerve to pray for her in a public fashion. I would just rub her forehead for a couple seconds with my finger as a stand-in for all those who were praying for her. I felt as though I was the little finger of the wider Body of Christ. The Church was praying, and I was the witness.

On my last day on the job, I went up to visit Anna, and her bed was empty. My first thought was, "She's dead." But I had to find out what had happened. So, I found her nurse and asked. Her response?

"Oh, she's off her morphine and IVs, and she's downstairs playing."

"Wow," I thought. "That's great! When do her skin grafts begin?

"Oh, she won't need any skin grafts." replied the nurse.

"Not even on her legs?" I asked because her legs had been really bad.

"Not even on her legs." she responded cheerfully.

I thought frantically: "Third-degree burns only heal on the edges. The burned skin must be replaced by grafts. No skin grafts meant that either she had been misdiagnosed originally or her skin had somehow regenerated." Under the circumstances, I thought I'd put my next question with considerable delicacy. "Isn't this a little unusual?" I asked cautiously.

"Oh yes, we're surprised," the nurse said. "Of course, we could have misdiagnosed her, but, boy, she looked charred when she came in."

I went downstairs and told my supervisor what they had told me upstairs. She was a lapsed Catholic who knew the story of this little girl and that we had been praying for her. She listened carefully and then said, "I think we know that something more than mere medicine has been at work here." Then she added wryly, "Maybe we should just hire you and let you wander the halls."

She thought — and I hoped — that this was a sign that I had been given the charism of Healing. I now know (after considerable discernment) that is not the case. I had witnessed the power of another kind of healing charism — intercessory prayer — flowing through hundreds of disciples. I was given the immense privilege of receiving a glimpse of what God can do through his people when they offer themselves and their charisms *together* as a channel of his purposes.

Before we can offer our charisms together, we have to be clear about what we mean by the term, "charism":

> "Charism" is the transcription of the Greek word *chárisma*, which, found frequently in the Pauline letters, also appears in the first letter of Peter. This term has a general sense of "generous gift" and, in the New Testament, is used only in reference to the divine gifts.... Unlike the fundamental graces such as sanctifying grace, or the gifts of faith, of hope, and of charity, that are indispensable for every Christian, an individual charism need not be a gift given to all (cf. 1 Cor 12:30). The charisms are particular gifts that the Spirit distributes "as He wishes" (1 Cor 12:11).[1]

---

[1] Letter *"Iuvenescit Ecclesia"* to the Bishops of the Catholic Church Regarding the Relationship Between Hierarchical and Charismatic Gifts in the Life and the Mission of the Church, 4, Congregation for Doctrine of the Faith, May, 2016 (online at http://www.vatican.va/roman_curia/congregations /cfaith/documents/rc_con_cfaith_doc_20160516_iuvenescit-ecclesia_ en.html, as of May 5, 2017).

It has been fascinating to discover that the charisms are as old as the Church and have been part of Catholic Tradition since her very beginning. The New Testament refers to them at some length in Romans 12, 1 Corinthians 12-14, Ephesians 4:7-16, and 1 Peter 4:10-11. The early Church Fathers and later theologians wrote about charisms extensively. Pre-Vatican II sources about the charisms include the *Didache*, St. Ignatius of Antioch, *The Shepherd of Hermas*, St. Justin Martyr, St. Irenaeus, Tertullian, Origen, Eusebius, St. Hilary of Poitiers, St. Cyril of Jerusalem, St. Basil the Great, St. Gregory of Nazianzus, the *Apostolic Constitutions*, St. John Chrysostom, St. Thomas Aquinas, and Pope Pius XII.

WHAT IS THE DIFFERENCE BETWEEN SANCTIFYING GIFTS AND CHARISMS?

In the New Testament, the word "charism" was originally used broadly. By the fourth century, the term was understood in the narrower and more defined sense than we use it now. In the thirteenth century, St. Thomas Aquinas stated clearly the Church's distinction between sanctifying grace (*gratia gratum faciens* — grace given for the good of the receiver) and "gratuitous" grace (*gratia gratis data* — grace given for the good of others). The charisms are gratuitous graces. Thomas writes:

> And thus there is a twofold grace: one whereby man himself is united to God, and this is called "sanctifying grace"; the other is that whereby one man cooperates with another in leading him to God, and this gift is called "gratuitous grace," since it is bestowed on a man beyond the capability of nature, and beyond the merit of the person. But whereas it is bestowed on a man, not

to justify him, but rather that he may cooperate in the justification of another, it is not called sanctifying grace. And it is of this that the Apostle says (1 Corinthians 12:7): "And the manifestation of the Spirit is given to every man unto utility," i.e., of others.[2]

The sanctifying gifts of the Spirit are much more than seven names that generations of Catholic children had to memorize: wisdom, understanding, counsel, knowledge, fortitude, piety, and fear of the Lord. The sanctifying gifts are given to us in baptism and sealed in confirmation. They are for us to keep. These gifts make us docile to the promptings of the Holy Spirit and help us to grow in holiness and to become ready for heaven. The sanctifying gifts are essential to our salvation, but they are *not* charisms.

Charisms are ultimately intended for other people, not ourselves, and do *not* convey sanctifying grace. To put it very simply, charisms are gifts of the Holy Spirit that we are given so that we can give them away. Charisms are graces that pass through you and me — with our cooperation — to convey God's truth, beauty, provision, healing, and mercy to someone else (see CCC 799). Charisms don't belong to us; we are merely their stewards. The manifestation of the charisms is one of the major ways that the presence and work of the Holy Spirit is revealed to us in this life.[3]

> [G]race also includes the gifts that the Spirit grants us to associate us with his work, to enable us to collaborate in the salvation of others and in the growth of the

---

[2] St. Thomas Aquinas, *Summa Theologiae*, I-II, 111, a1 (available online at http://www.newadvent.org/summa/2111.htm#article1, as of May 5, 2017).

[3] CCC 688 and Pope St. John Paul II, *Redemptoris Missio* ("Mission of the Redeemer"), 18 (online at http://w2.vatican.va/content/john-paul-ii/en /encyclicals/documents/hf_jp-ii_enc_07121990_redemptoris-missio.html, as of May 5, 2017).

Body of Christ, the Church.... There are furthermore *special graces*, also called *charisms* after the Greek term used by St. Paul and meaning "favor," "gratuitous gift," "benefit." Whatever their character ... charisms are oriented toward sanctifying grace and are intended for the common good of the Church. They are at the service of charity which builds up the Church. (CCC 2003, emphasis in original)

It is important to remember that manifesting a charism is *not* necessarily a sign of holiness or a guarantee that the one exercising the gift is a saint. Nonetheless, through the charisms, God can use us to remove impediments to faith and open other people's hearts and minds to that which does convey sanctifying grace. That is why Paul also says, "Pursue love, but strive eagerly for the spiritual gifts" (1 Corinthians 14:1).

CHARISMS ARE GIVEN TO ALL THE BAPTIZED FOR THE SAKE OF MISSION

The Church, from St. Paul to the Second Vatican Council, teaches that charisms are given to all the baptized. *Lumen Gentium* asserts that "the manifestation of the Spirit is given to everyone for profit,"[4] while *Ad Gentes* says this:

The Christian faithful, having different gifts (cf. Rom 12:6), according to each one's opportunity, ability, charisms and ministry (cf. 1 Cor 3:10) must all cooperate in the Gospel. Hence all alike, those who sow and those who reap (cf. Jn 4:37), those who plant and those who irrigate, must be one (cf. 1 Cor 3:8), so that

---

[4] *Lumen Gentium*, 12.

"in a free and orderly fashion cooperating toward the same end," they may spend their forces harmoniously for the building up of the Church.[5]

Following *Lumen Gentium* (nn. 12-13), Pope St. John Paul II in *Christifideles Laici* insists on the importance of this distribution of charisms to all the baptized because every baptized person has a "*totally unique contribution*" to make[6] to the Church's mission:

> The Spirit of the Lord gives a vast variety of charisms, inviting people to assume different ministries and forms of service and reminding them, as he reminds all people in their relationship in the Church, that what distinguishes persons is *not an increase in dignity*, but *a special and complementary capacity for service....* Thus, the charisms, the ministries, the different forms of service exercised by the lay faithful exist in communion and on behalf of communion. They are treasures that complement one another for the good of all and are under the wise guidance of their Pastors."[7]

So that she can fulfill her mission, the Holy Spirit "bestows upon [the Church] varied hierarchic and charismatic gifts, and in this way directs her."[8]

---

[5] *Ad Gentes* (Decree on the Missionary Activity of the Church), 28 (online at http://www.vatican.va/archive/hist_councils/ii_vatican_council/documents /vat-ii_decree_19651207_ad-gentes_en.html, as of May 5, 2017).

[6] Pope St. John Paul II, *Christifideles Laici*, 20, emphasis in original.

[7] Ibid., emphasis in original.

[8] CCC 768. See also Pope Blessed Paul VI, *Evangelii Nuntiandi* (on evangelization in the modern world), 74 (online at http://w2.vatican.va /content/paul-vi/en/apost_exhortations/documents/hf_p-vi_exh_19751208_ evangelii-nuntiandi.html, as of May 5, 2017); *Ad Gentes*, 4; Pope St. John Paul II, *Redemptoris Missio*, 18; and *Iuvenescit Ecclesia*, 15.

How Many Charisms Are There?

One question that people often ask is, "How many kinds of charisms are there?"

The simple answer is, "We don't know." There is no definitive list in either the Scriptures, the early Fathers, or any magisterial authority — which shouldn't surprise us. Charisms are gifts from an infinitely creative God. As St. Irenaeus wrote in about the year 180, "It is not possible to name the number of the gifts which the Church, [scattered] throughout the whole world, has received from God...."[9]

There are charisms listed in Scripture and the Fathers of the Church that we don't discuss in the course of the Called & Gifted workshop because our time is limited. We cover twenty-three of the most common charisms in the course of the workshop. If Called & Gifted participants have questions about other gifts, we help people discern those gifts as well. Our working list of charisms includes:

- Encouragement
- Helps
- Hospitality
- Mercy
- Pastoring
- Evangelism
- Prophecy
- Teaching
- Administration
- Leadership
- Giving
- Service

---

[9] St. Irenaeus, *Against Heresies*, 2:32, 4 (online at http://www.newadvent.org /fathers/0103232.htm, as of May 5, 2017).

- Celibacy
- Extraordinary Faith
- Missionary
- Voluntary Poverty
- Healing
- Intercessory Prayer
- Knowledge
- Wisdom
- Craftsmanship
- Music
- Writing

As you can see, our list includes some charisms that people tend to think of as dramatic and extraordinary, such as Healing and Prophecy, and others that seem so ordinary — Service or Hospitality — that some are surprised they are charisms at all. I will go over the characteristics of these charisms in some detail later.

A Brief History of Charisms

In the early Church, charisms were understood to be given by the Holy Spirit when adults were baptized. Tertullian wrote the very first treatise on the sacrament of Baptism about A.D. 200. He described what he would tell adults about to be baptized and confirmed:

> Therefore, you blessed ones, for whom the grace of God is waiting, when you come up from the most sacred bath of the new birth, when you spread out your hands for the first time in your mother's house with your brethren, ask your Father, ask your Lord, for the special

gift of his inheritance, the distributed charisms, which form an additional underlying feature [of baptism]. Ask, he says, and you shall receive. In fact, you have sought, and you have found: you have knocked, and it has been opened to you.[10]

A century and a half later, charisms were still seen as normative in the life of the newly baptized. In the year 348, St. Cyril, the bishop of Jerusalem, spoke to adults about to be baptized at Easter and described the Holy Spirit distributing the charisms to the baptized throughout the world:

Consider, I pray, of each nation, Bishops, Presbyters, Deacons, Solitaries, Virgins, and laity besides; and then behold their great Protector, and the Dispenser of their gifts; how throughout the world He gives to one chastity, to another perpetual virginity, to another almsgiving, to another voluntary poverty, to another power of repelling hostile spirits.[11]

And he adds:

For it is one and the Self-same Spirit who divides His gifts to every man severally as He will (1 Corinthians 12:11) Himself the while remaining undivided.[12]

Cyril did not know it, but he was living in the midst of a major sociological shift in the life of the Church. Forty years

---

[10] Tertullian, *On Baptism*, 20 (adapted from online at http://www.newadvent .org/fathers/0321.htm, as of May 5, 2017).

[11] St. Cyril of Jerusalem, *Catechetical Lectures*, 16:22 (online at http://www .newadvent.org/fathers/310116.htm, as of May 5, 2017).

[12] Ibid., 17:2 (online at http://www.newadvent.org/fathers/310117.htm, as of May 5, 2017).

after that Easter in Jerusalem, theologians were lamenting that the charisms had become a much rarer experience in the life of the Christian community. Why?

In 313, Christianity was legalized in the Roman Empire. The emperor Constantine was baptized on his deathbed twenty-four years later. In 380, Catholic Christianity was declared to be the state religion of the Roman Empire. As the political pendulum swung decisively in favor of the Church, many Roman citizens sought baptism and the Church grew dramatically in a single century. In short, the Church moved from being persecuted to being politically powerful. But in the process, the Church was also swamped with nominal Christians who chose baptism simply because they wanted to be on the winning side.

These developments triggered what we now think of as the monastic movement. Serious disciples went out from the cities into the desert, seeking what they called "green martyrdom." Since Christians were no longer being martyred in the cities, the desert fathers and mothers moved out into the wilderness where they formed monastic communities devoted to prayer, fasting, penance, study, and care for the poor.

The result of this split between nominal Christians in the cities and a growing movement of dedicated ascetics outside the cities was that, over time, serious discipleship, devotion, and apostolic initiative became firmly associated with an ascetic life and monasticism, while the life of ordinary Christians in the cities was perceived as compromised. Among the teeming throngs of nominal Christians who filled the urban areas, the charisms began to disappear but continued to be manifested in the new monastic communities.

Cyril of Jerusalem was speaking of charisms as normative in 348. By 386, in Antioch, St. John Chrysostom was lamenting their apparent disappearance as he looked back wistfully on the recent past when they were normative:

For in truth the Church was a heaven then, the Spirit governing all things, and moving each one of the rulers and making him inspired. But now we retain only the symbols of those gifts.... But the present Church is like a woman who has fallen from her former prosperous days, and in many respects retains the symbols only of that ancient prosperity; displaying indeed the repositories and caskets of her golden ornaments, but bereft of her wealth: such a one does the present Church resemble.[13]

That was the beginning of a widespread working assumption that did not reflect formal Church teaching but came to dominate Catholic thought and practice for the next fourteen centuries. Charisms, vocations, and a sense of apostolic mission came to be seen as rare and as signs of extraordinary sanctity or of a call to priesthood or religious life. For instance, even as late as the early twentieth century, a common assumption was that only a nun or priest would be called to the apostolate of working directly with the poor.

One of Canada's great lay apostles, Catherine Doherty, challenged the power of this cultural assumption. When Catherine started a personal outreach to the poor in Toronto in 1930, the lay Catholics around her were taken aback. She was neither a priest nor a sister, so how dare she undertake an initiative like this? When Catherine felt a strong desire to move into the slums and live a life of voluntary poverty and service to the poor, her archbishop told her that her idea was fifty years ahead of its time.[14]

---

[13] St. John Chrysostom, *On 1 Corinthians, Homily 36*, 14:33 (online at http://www.newadvent.org/fathers/220136.htm, as of May 5, 2017).

[14] Lorene Hanley Duquin, *They Called Her the Baroness: The Life of Catherine de Hueck Doherty* (New York: Alba House, 1995), pp. 122-123.

Although they were profoundly different in personality, Catherine and Dorothy Day were friends and comrades engaged in pioneering lay apostolates with the poor. They were especially close during the 1940s when their respective apostolates were both located in New York City. As Catherine put it later:

> When I moved to Harlem, Dorothy Day and I became even closer ... occasionally when we both had enough money, let's say about a dollar, we would go to Child's where you could get three coffee refills ... and we used to enjoy each cup and just talk.
>
> Talk about God. Talk about the apostolate. Talk about all the things that were dear to our hearts. But we were both very lonely because, believe it or not, there were just the two of us in all of Canada and America, and we did feel lonely and no question about it. Periodically we would have a good cry in our coffee cups. We really cried, I mean honest, big tears ... Dorothy and I would hold hands, and we would cry. We had had it! But we would always rally.[15]

While Catherine and Dorothy were commiserating over their coffee, Pope Pius XII was meditating on theological developments that would bring them much comfort and support. In his 1943 document *Mystici Corporis Christi* (on the mystery of the mystical Body of Christ), the pope dealt, in part, with the relationship and necessity of both the hierarchical and the charismatic dimensions of the Church:

---

[15] Restoration, February 1981 (online at http://www.madonnahouse.org /restoration/2008/09/dorothy_day_and_catherine_dohe.html, as of May 5, 2017).

One must not think, however, that this ordered or "organic" structure of the body of the Church contains only hierarchical elements and with them is complete; or, as an opposite opinion holds, that it is composed only of those who enjoy charismatic gifts — though members gifted with miraculous powers will never be lacking in the Church.[16]

The pope was challenging two equal and opposite errors. The first was the clericalist notion that "the Church" is only made up of the clergy (and secondarily non-ordained religious), which was surprisingly widespread before the Second Vatican Council. The second was the anti-clericalist notion that the only real Christians are those who manifest various charismatic gifts. This was part of Pius XII's larger re-evaluation of the responsibilities and mission of the laity:

Within the Church, there exist not an active and passive element, leadership and lay people. All members of the Church are called to work on the perfection of the body of Christ. ... Lay believers are in the front line of Church life; for them the Church is the animating principle of human society. Therefore, they in particular ought to have an ever-clearer consciousness not only of belonging to the Church, but of being the Church, that is to say, the community of the faithful on earth under the leadership of the Pope, the common Head, and of the bishops in communion with him. They are the Church.[17]

---

[16] Pope Pius XII, *Mystici Corporis Christi* (on the Mystical Body of Christ), 17, June 29, 1943 (online at http://w2.vatican.va/content/pius-xii/en/encyclicals /documents/hf_p-xii_enc_29061943_mystici-corporis-christi.html, as of May 5, 2017).

[17] Pope Pius XII, Discourse (February 20, 1946): AAS 38 (1946) 149; quoted by Pope St. John Paul II, *Christifideles Laici*, 9.

It all set the stage for the debates at Vatican II. By 1962, the Church found itself in a situation much more like that of the early Church than that of Christendom. It had become a minority voice in a secular world that was ignorant of, indifferent to, or openly hostile to the faith. In such an environment, the missionary importance of the charisms was recovered for the whole Church.

Vatican II: A Watershed in the Theology of Charisms

It was in this context that the council fathers held the first conciliar discussion on the role of the laity and the charisms in history during its October 1963 debate over the draft of *Lumen Gentium*. At issue was the place of the laity in the Church's mission, and since charisms are vital to the accomplishment of that mission, they were part of that discussion. In its final form, *Lumen Gentium* would reaffirm in ringing tones the teaching of the Church stretching back to the New Testament itself:

> It is not only through the sacraments and the ministries of the Church that the Holy Spirit sanctifies and leads the people of God and enriches it with virtues, but, "allotting His gifts to everyone according as He wills" (1 Cor 12:11), He distributes special graces among the faithful of every rank. By these gifts He makes them fit and ready to undertake the various tasks and offices which contribute toward the renewal and building up of the Church, according to the words of the Apostle: "The manifestation of the Spirit is given to everyone for profit" (cf. 1 Thess 5:12, 9-21). These charisms, whether they be the more outstanding or the more simple and

widely diffused, are to be received with thanksgiving and consolation for they are perfectly suited to and useful for the needs of the Church.[18]

Popes John Paul II and Benedict XVI both built on this foundation. Pope St. John Paul II asserted clearly that the charismatic dimension of the Church is "co-essential" with the institutional dimension:

> [T]here is no conflict or opposition in the Church between the *institutional dimension* and the *charismatic dimension*, of which movements are a significant expression. Both are co-essential to the divine constitution of the Church founded by Jesus, because they both help to make the mystery of Christ and his saving work present in the world.[19]

Pope Benedict XVI, in addition to confirming the co-essentiality of the gifts, deepened the affirmation of his predecessor, writing that "in the Church the essential institutions are also charismatic."[20] In short, there is no part of the Church that is simply institutional and devoid of the charismatic. There is no such thing as a "charism-free zone" within the Church.

THREE TYPES OF CHARISMS

There are three basic types of charisms in the Church's understanding: *individual, founding*, and *hierarchical*. I will be discuss-

---

[18] *Lumen Gentium*, 12.

[19] Pope St. John Paul II, *Message of Pope John Paul II for the World Congress of Ecclesial Movements and New Communities*, May 27, 1998, emphasis in original (online at https://w2.vatican.va/content/john-paul-ii/en /speeches/1998/may/documents/hf_jp-ii_spe_19980527_movimenti.html, as of May 5, 2017).

[20] *Iuvenescit Ecclesia*, 10.

ing individual charisms in great detail in the rest of the book, but in this chapter I will also provide a brief introduction to the *founding* and *hierarchical* charisms.

What does the Church teach about the charisms given to individual believers?

1. They are given to all the baptized since they are part of the gift of the Holy Spirit.
2. All charisms are to be received with "thanksgiving and consolation."[21] We are not to recoil from them in embarrassment, reject them as a "Protestant thing," nor ignore them in false humility.
3. "[E]ach person is required first to have a knowledge and discernment of his or her own charisms and those of others."[22] Interestingly, although this sentence comes from a document written to clergy, it clearly applies to all the baptized since it speaks of "his or her" charisms. The priest is to be strengthened by all the charisms that surround him.
4. Each believer has the "right and duty" to use their charisms in the Church and in the world for the good of others. This should be done by the laity in communion with their brothers in Christ, especially with their pastors who must make a judgment about the true nature and proper use of these gifts not to extinguish the Spirit but to test all things and hold for what is good.[23]

Note that the language about the "right and duty" of all the believers to use their charisms is exactly the same language that the Church uses in connection

[21] *Lumen Gentium*, 12.

[22] Pope St. John Paul II, *Pastores Dabo Vobis*, 31.

[23] See *Apostolicam Actuositatem*, 3.

with the formation of seminarians in preparation for ordination.[24] It would be unimaginable now for a priest to be ordained without extensive seminary formation. *It should likewise be unimaginable that the local Christian community — the parish — is not a house of apostolic formation for all the baptized and a place where they can discern and be encouraged to exercise their charisms in the whole of their life.*

5. The charisms "lavished" on the baptized call each individual to be "active and co-responsible."[25] There is no place for passivity in the Kingdom. We are to welcome and "exercise our charisms as part of taking seriously our co-responsibility for the mission of the Church.

6. The gifts "demand" that those who have received them "exercise them" for the growth of the whole Church. We are to be "good stewards" of the graces given us.[26]

7. Charisms enable each member of the faithful to offer a "totally unique contribution."[27] There is something you and I have been given to do and to give that no one else in the entire Church can do or give.

8. "Each one, therefore, must be helped to embrace the gift entrusted to him as a completely unique person, and to hear the words which the Spirit of

---

[24] See Congregation for the Clergy, *Directory for the Ministry and the Life of Priests, New Edition* (Vatican: Libreria Editrice Vaticana, 2013), 90 (online at http://www.clerus.org/clerus/dati/2013-06/13-13/Direttorio_EN.pdf, as of May 5, 2017).

[25] Pope St. John Paul II, *Christifideles Laici*, 21.

[26] Ibid., 24.

[27] Ibid., 20.

God personally addresses to him."[28] The Christian community is called to help all Catholics embrace those gifts and use them for the good of all.

9. The discernment of charisms is always necessary. No charism is exempt from being referred and submitted to the Church's shepherds.[29]

FOUNDING CHARISMS

A recent document from the Congregation for the Doctrine of the Faith tells us:

Among the charismatic gifts, freely distributed by the Holy Spirit, many are received and lived out by persons within the Christian community who have no need of particular regulations. When, however, a gift presents itself as a *"founding"* or *"originating charism,"* this requires a specific recognition so that the richness it contains may be adequately articulated within the ecclesial communion and faithfully transmitted over time. *Here emerges the decisive task of discernment that appertains to the ecclesial authorities.*[30]

Founding charisms are sometimes also called "originating" or "group" charisms. They are *not* the same as individual charisms. Although individual charisms require the support and oversight of the Church in the course of discernment, these gifts are exercised by the laity with no direct ecclesial oversight unless they are being used in a formal parish or diocesan

---

[28] Pope St. John Paul II, *Pastores Dabo Vobis*, 40.
[29] See CCC 801 and Pope John Paul II, *Christifideles Laici*, 24.
[30] *Iuvenescit Ecclesia*, 17, emphasis added.

setting. The vast majority of individual charisms are exercised by mature disciples in the workplace as well as at home as part of day-to-day life. You do not have to call your pastor or bishop to get permission to exercise your charism of Mercy and buy lunch for a homeless mom and her children!

But founding charisms always involve a vision of how God is calling a *group* of Christians together to commit to a particular focus on the Gospel, a particular kind of Christian spirituality, a communal way of life, and a particular ecclesial mission. When Ignatius of Loyola or Mother Teresa were called to found a stable community dedicated to a particular kind of spirituality and role in the Church's mission, they were exercising a founding charism, and it is crucial that the Church carefully discern whether this is merely a human activity or something that God is establishing because "Unless the Lord build the house, they labor in vain who build" (Psalms 127:1). At the same time, the Church needs to be careful not to quench the Spirit (see 1 Thessalonians 5:19):

> Ecclesial movements and new communities show how a determinate founding charism can gather the faithful together and help them to live fully their Christian vocation and proper state of life in service of the ecclesial mission."[31]

> [T]here is the need for *fidelity to the founding charism* and subsequent spiritual heritage of each Institute. It is precisely in this fidelity to the inspiration of the founders and foundresses, an inspiration which is itself a gift of the Holy Spirit, that the essential elements of

---

[31] Ibid., 16.

the consecrated life can be more readily discerned and more fervently put into practice.[32]

The fathers of the Second Vatican Council strongly encouraged established religious communities to contemplate again the founding charism of their community to see if they had remained true to their call. That is why Pope St. John Paul II continues:

> Important elements enabling Institutes to play a successful part in new evangelization are fidelity to the founding charism, communion with all those who in the Church are involved in the same undertaking, especially the Bishops, and cooperation with all people of good will.[33]

An illustration of this principle being consciously applied by a religious order can be seen in the Dominican Sisters of Presentation's discussion of their own charism:

> The Charism gives birth to the Institution. The Charism is lived in time and space through the Institution. A founding Charism, such as the one of Marie Poussepin, has in an intrinsic manner, the capacity for institutionalization that enables it to exist. The structure determines the way in which the Charism is to be lived in the Church and its organization respond to the laws which guide it. Reciprocal duties and rights spring forth from

---

[32] Pope St. John Paul II, *Vita Consecrata* ("The Consecrated Life"), 36, emphasis in original (online at http://w2.vatican.va/content/john-paul-ii/en/apost_exhortations/documents/hf_jp-ii_exh_25031996_vita-consecrata.html, as of May 5, 2017).

[33] Ibid., 81.

the founding Charism. They are morally binding and ensure the continuity of the Institution and its capacity to adapt to historical circumstances.[34]

What is essential in a founding charism is that the gift calls others to a particular, stable, and communal Christian spirituality, a common life, and a specific mission. One test is whether or not the call results in the establishment of a new missional Christian community sustained by established structures and spiritual practices and explicitly recognized by the Church. Therefore, Pope St. John Paul II says:

> The Spirit, who at different times has inspired numerous forms of consecrated life, does not cease to assist the Church, whether by fostering in already existing Institutes a commitment to renewed faithfulness to the founding charism, or by giving new charisms to men and women of our own day so that they can start institutions responding to the challenges of our times.[35]

A founder or foundress of a group usually has individual charisms that are *not* passed on to the community as part of the founding charism. When I first read the life of St. Dominic, I noticed that he appeared to have had a personal charism of Administration. But Dominicans will tell you that administration is not the strong suit of most Dominicans! And that's okay because Dominic's individual charism was not an essential part of the community's founding charism: preaching

---

[34] Dominican Sisters of Presentation (online at https://www.domipresen.com /index.php/en/about-us/our-identity/charism, as of May 5, 2017).

[35] Pope St. John Paul II, *Vita Consecrata*, 62.

that makes the saving truth of the Gospel of Jesus Christ better and more widely known.[36]

Those who are called by God to participate in the founding charism of a particular group will also have their own individual charisms that contribute to and are expressed in the context of the larger community. So, it is not uncommon for members of religious congregations and lay movements to have individual charisms that may vary significantly from the founding charism of their community and which will color and empower how individual members live out the communal charism.

This distinction between a person's individual charisms and the founding charism of the community to which he or she belongs can also be a possible source of healthy tension. I mention this tension because sometimes individual community members can conclude that this tension means that they made a mistake in discernment. In fact, a genuine vocation to a specific religious community can co-exist with the fact that a member brings a different kind of fruitfulness to the community via the exercise of a contrasting individual charism. So, for instance, a Dominican with an individual charism of Healing can bring to his order an informed insight on healing ministry that can be a focus of his writing and preaching, as it was for Father Leo Thomas, O.P.[37]

HIERARCHICAL CHARISMS

Finally, there is the phenomenon of hierarchical charisms in the life of the Church. These are gifts that come with the sacrament of Holy Orders. They include:

---

[36] See *Dominican Charism*, Order of Preachers (online at http://www.op.org/en /content/dominican-charism, as of May 5, 2017).

[37] See Leo Thomas, O.P. and Jan Alkire, *Healing Ministry: A Practical Guide* (New York: Sheed & Ward, 1994).

1. "[T]he institution of the Eucharist (cf. Lk 22:19f.; 1 Cor 11:25), the power to forgive sins (cf. Jn 20:22f.), the apostolic mandate for the work of evangelization and of baptism (Mc 16:15f; Mt 28:18-20) — primarily appears in the hierarchical gifts, in as much as they pertain to the sacrament of Orders."[38]
2. The charism of Infallibility exercised in different ways by the Pope and bishops (see CCC 890-892).
3. The reality that "every priest receives his vocation from our Lord through the Church as a gracious gift, a grace *gratis data* (charisma)."[39]
4. The grace of perfect chastity in priestly celibacy.[40] (It should be noted that the Church does not teach that the reception of holy orders *confers* the charism of Celibacy. Whether or not the grace of celibacy is already in place must be discerned before a man is ordained.)

Those who possess hierarchical charisms because they are ordained are also given various individual charisms that need to be discerned and will significantly affect and color how they live out their priestly vocation. The relationship between hierarchical and charismatic gifts is directed to the "full participation of the faithful in her communion and evangelizing mission."[41]

CLAIMING OUR BIRTHRIGHT

Paul prays for all baptized Christians:

---

[38] *Iuvenescit Ecclesia*, 12.
[39] Pope St. John Paul II, *Pastores Dabo Vobis*, 35.
[40] Ibid., 29.
[41] *Iuvenescit Ecclesia*, 13.

... that you may know what is the hope that belongs to his call, what are the riches of glory in his inheritance among the holy ones, and what is the surpassing greatness of his power for us who believe, in accord with the exercise of his great might. (Ephesians 1:18-19)

In the *Catechism*, there is a wonderful section regarding the "Communion in Spiritual Goods," which includes the "communion of charisms":

Within the communion of the Church, the Holy Spirit "distributes special graces among the faithful of every rank" for the building up of the Church. Now, "to each is given the manifestation of the Spirit for the common good." (CCC 951)

Not only are individual charisms found widely distributed throughout the Church, but the fruit they bear belongs to all of us. It is time to take a more detailed look at some specific charisms and begin to explore the riches of our inheritance.

CHAPTER 5

Charisms 101

Pursue love, but strive eagerly for the spiritual gifts.

1 CORINTHIANS 14:1

In the last chapter, I briefly outlined the difference between *founding, hierarchical,* and *individual* charisms. From here on out, when I use the word "charism," remember that I am talking only about *individual* charisms. The discernment and impact of individual charisms has been one of the major focuses of our work at the Catherine of Siena Institute for the past twenty years.

The *Catechism* speaks of the baptism of Jesus in the River Jordan in these terms:

> Then the Holy Spirit, in the form of a dove, comes upon Jesus and a voice from heaven proclaims, "This is my beloved Son." This is the manifestation ("Epiphany") of Jesus as Messiah of Israel and Son of God. (CCC 535)

Manifestation, or Epiphany, refers to the public revelation of what was *present already but hidden.* Jesus possessed the Holy Spirit in fullness from his conception, but the manifestation of the Spirit's presence happened *publicly* at his baptism.

In a similar way, you and I received the Holy Spirit in our baptism. I sometimes have to reassure people there is no such thing as a validly baptized person who has not received the Holy

Spirit. But the public *manifestation* of the Holy Spirit through fruit-bearing, including the exercise of our charisms and the living of our vocations, requires intentional cooperation on our part. Grace is not irresistible. We must choose in faith to do what God has called and anointed us to do. What baptism planted in us like seeds underground in a Rocky Mountain winter will begin to grow and become visible to us and to the world when we respond to the call of Jesus with faith and obedience.

It cannot be stressed enough that charisms and vocations are *supernatural* realities that manifest out of an individual's sustained relationship with Jesus. We have met Catholic pastoral leaders who presume that "charism" is just the latest religious word for *natural* talents or strengths and a quick way to meet obvious institutional needs. But charisms are *not* natural human abilities or strengths and *not* given just so that we can be volunteers at the parish for a couple of hours or even so we can be effective full-time staff.

Charisms are supernaturally empowered graces given to apostles who have a mission to bring the presence and love of Jesus Christ to a specific setting or situation. Charisms are *whole-life gifts* that apostles take with them everywhere they go. We are called to exercise them at work, with family and friends, and in the broader community, as well as in the parish or diocese. The vast majority of lay Catholics will exercise their apostolate primarily in the secular sphere — therefore the exercise of their charisms takes place outside as well as within the Christian community.

WHEN DO CHARISMS EMERGE IN OUR LIVES?

Charisms typically manifest *after* the point in our lives when our faith becomes active and personal — usually after we reach the threshold of intentional discipleship. Charisms typically begin to manifest within a year or two after a conversion or spiritual awakening.

Thousands of people have told us stories:

> I went through a conversion last year and then this stuff began to happen. My friend's father was depressed. He disappeared suddenly and my friend was afraid that his dad might commit suicide. I had this strong sense that we could help his dad by praying so I asked a group of friends to come together to pray for him. We prayed and my friend's dad suddenly felt better and decided to return home the next day.

Or there is this story:

> I came back to faith after a friend invited me to a parish evangelization retreat three years ago. After that, so much changed. Last year, I felt this intense desire to get involved in my parish's St. Vincent de Paul Society and one thing led to another. Now I'm working on plans to start a shelter for battered women! I've never done anything like this before. My friends wonder what happened to me.

These kinds of experiences are classic signs of an emerging post-conversion charism. When I am in the middle of what we call "gifts interviews," I typically ask the individual I am working with to briefly tell me the story of their relationship with God. What I'm listening for is a significant turning point — a spiritual awakening or conversion experience — because their charisms will usually begin to manifest after that point in their life. It saves us both a lot of time if I know that they went through a conversion five years ago because now I know the most likely period in which to look for the manifestation of a charism.

THE NEEDS OF OTHERS CALL FORTH OUR CHARISMS

Charisms also tend to manifest for the first time when we meet the person or situation that needs the gift because charisms are always for others. Until we meet the person with the need that God has anointed us to fill, we may not manifest that particular charism. For this reason, it can take years for all the charisms given to an individual to manifest.

For instance, St. Francis Xavier is the patron saint of missionaries, but his missionary career began "accidentally" when another Jesuit fell ill and Francis took his place on twenty-four-hours' notice. His charism of Missionary, which empowered him to use his other charisms in a culture not his own, manifested when he was around people who needed it:

> Francis Xavier believed no one was more ill-equipped than he to take the Gospel overseas. But he was wrong....
>
> Some believe that Francis Xavier had a miraculous gift of languages, which enabled him to communicate fluently with everyone, but that was not the case. Francis struggled with foreign languages and was barely able to express the creed, commandments, and prayers in Tamil and other native languages.... The real miracle of tongues was that Xavier spread the Gospel so far and to so many with such little grasp of their languages.[1]

So, it is common that those who are young in their Christian life or have a limited life experience may have charisms

---

[1] Bert Ghezzi, *Mystics & Miracles: True Stories of Lives Touched by God* (Chicago: Loyola, 2004). Excerpt from "Saint Francis Xavier, 1506-1552" (online at http://www.loyolapress.com/our-catholic-faith/saints/saints -stories-for-all-ages/saint-francis-xavier-1506-1552, as of May 5, 2017).

they don't know about yet because they haven't manifested yet. If that is the case, it is important for the discerner to explore new situations or get involved in new ministry or creative work that attracts them, and see what emerges.

WHAT ABOUT NON-CATHOLICS, BOTH BAPTIZED AND NON-BAPTIZED?

Bottom line: Baptism guarantees that we have received graces from the Holy Spirit. If someone is validly baptized — whether Catholic or not — we know that they have been given charisms along with the presence of the Holy Spirit, even if nothing has manifested yet. So when Catholics tell me they have no charisms, I simply ask, "Are you baptized?" If they say, "Yes," the most truthful response is a playful one: "It's too late."

The faith of the Church is also that, while *we* are bound by the sacraments, God is not bound (CCC 1257). Therefore, he can distribute charisms to anyone he pleases. This idea is not a new one. St. Justin Martyr, for instance, argued that the Logos, the Second Person of the Trinity, inspired Socrates with wisdom to refute his enemies.[2] Therefore, *unbaptized people may also be given charisms, but there is no way to know for sure until the gift manifests.* The presence of charisms in an unbaptized person's life is totally dependent upon their living relationship with God and their desire to be an instrument of his love for others.

I once had a young woman come up to me during the first break in a Called & Gifted workshop I was teaching. She asked, "Can I have one of those?"

I said, "Do you mean a charism?"

---

[2] St. Justin Martyr, *First Apology*, 5 (online at http://www.newadvent.org /fathers/0126.htm, as of May 5, 2017).

She said, "Yes! But I have to tell you: I'm Jewish. I'm not baptized. I'm not planning on being baptized."

I had to ask, "Okay. Here's my question for you: Do you want to be an instrument of God's love for someone else?"

She responded, "Absolutely!"

I said, "You're qualified."

Of course, I couldn't promise her that she *had* actually been given a charism, but I could tell her that she had the necessary disposition and desire to be used by God for the good of others. We went on to have a fascinating conversation about the Incarnation, and her beaming Catholic mother-in-law was standing behind her, so I guessed that this young woman was on a spiritual journey that she was not ready to put into words. The existence of the charisms and their part in the economy of redemption can easily spark spiritual trust and curiosity in people who come from non-Christian backgrounds.

WHAT DO ALL CHARISMS HAVE IN COMMON?

All the charisms are evangelizing in their own way because they make aspects of Jesus' redemptive work visible and accessible to others. Each charism conveys some portion of Jesus' grace and mercy to the world and points back to him. The charisms of Mercy, Music, even Administration reveal some facet of the light and power of Christ. That is why even unbelievers find the fruit of charisms attractive and compelling. Nevertheless, other people have to willingly receive the "good fruit" of your gift. They can choose to resist or reject the provision of God offered through your charism.

In a similar way, all the charisms are healing, because they make the love of God present, and where the love of God is present, healing occurs at some level. It may be obvious healing, such as dramatic physical healing at the hands of somebody with a charism of Healing, or it may be the healing of one's heart when a lonely person is welcomed into the home of somebody with a charism of Hospitality.

WHAT ARE THE CHARACTERISTICS OF AN INDIVIDUAL CHARISM?

Individual charisms have certain characteristics in common.

First of all, the kind of charism you can discern is given long-term. It is a way that God uses you over and over again for the sake of others. Because these gifts are long-term, you can recognize ongoing patterns in your life that indicate the presence of a charism.

You don't have to worry that God will arbitrarily change his mind in the middle of the night. You won't go to bed a happily married administrator but wake up the next morning to discover that you are now a celibate exorcist! Because of this stability, you can grow in the exercise of the charism as you grow spiritually, and your experience with and understanding of your charism can unfold, deepen, and mature over time. (There are temporary charisms too, and I will talk about them in a moment.)

Second, all the charisms have an impact for the Kingdom of God that goes above and beyond our natural abilities, skills, and purely human talents. There is a fruitfulness and impact for God's purposes that transcends what we can accomplish on our own.

Third, charisms are focused outward. They are always for others, not ourselves. Someone with a charism feels a desire to use it for others. You will be restless unless you can give the gift away. If you are comfortable using what you think may be a charism primarily or exclusively for your own benefit, then it is almost certainly not a spiritual gift but some kind of natural ability or learned skill. So, if you happen to like to crochet in the evenings to relax while you watch TV but have no interest in making things for other people, that's a hobby, not a charism.

I once did an interview with a woman who thought she might have a charism of Writing. Her prayer journals were full of wonderful stuff, she said. But when I asked her if she had shared her work with anybody else, she replied, "Are you kidding? That's private!" I had to tell her that until she could pluck up the courage to show her writing to others, there was simply no way to discern the presence of a charism.

Finally, charisms are received from God, not chosen by us. Over the years, I've had a number of people get angry with me and/or God because they didn't get the charism they wanted. God gives his gifts sovereignly for our particular mission in life, for our happiness, and for the ultimate happiness of others. You can always ask for a particular charism if you really believe you need it for the sake of people or situations around you. Jesus tells us to ask the Father for his good gifts (Matthew 7:7-11) and James says, "You do not possess because you do not ask" (James 4:2). But God may answer your prayer by making that charism available through someone else.

I've been there. I badly wanted the charism of Healing. So I asked God for it persistently. I read all the books and went to all the workshops. Then I worked my way through graduate school on an oncology unit. If I had a charism of Healing, I would know it by now. I was perfectly free to ask, and God responded: "I have something better for you. Trust me on this one: you're gonna like it." The bottom line is that while we can help one another discern what God has given to us, we cannot put in what God has left out.

Temporary Charisms

In addition to the long-term charisms, there are also *temporary* charisms. Any one of us, if we are available, can be used by God in a truly out-of-the-box way in a particular situation. Such charisms are given only for the moment and cannot be further developed. They are, if you will, "one-offs" that God in his inscrutable wisdom gives to a disciple for his own mysterious purposes and which might never occur again. The person in front of you has a need, and you are the available apostle in that place, so God gives you a temporary gift to meet the need.

Father Michael Sweeney had an experience like this years ago. He was scheduled to hear confessions at a young-adult retreat and was running a little late. When he got to his assigned place, there was a young woman already waiting for him, so he sat down and began hearing her confession. As he did so, a loud, persistent thought filled his mind: "Tell her to finish her book."

Father Michael said to himself, "I will *not!*" It felt absurd to say such a thing to a complete stranger. She'd think he was crazy. But the thought would not leave him alone and kept coming back, "Tell her to finish her book!" So after she had finished her confession and had received absolution, Father Michael tentatively said, "This may not make any sense to you, and I know this is unusual, but I have a strong sense that I'm supposed to tell you to finish your book."

She went white as a sheet. It turned out that her unfinished book was the biggest single issue in her life. But she had not associated it with sin, so she had not confessed it.

Afterward, Father Michael puzzled over this strange experience and wondered, "Why me? Why didn't God just tell her directly, 'Finish your book'?" But then it occurred to him that, in fact, God probably *had* told her, and she had responded with a litany of excuses like so many of us do: *I don't have anything to say. It's a stupid idea. Nobody will publish it. No one will read it,* etc. So God sent her a total stranger to tell her in a clear and unmistakable way to *finish her book.*

Understandably, Father Michael was braced for anything the next time he heard a confession. But it never happened again. For some, a charism of Prophecy is an ongoing pattern in their lives and can be discerned as a long-term gift. For Father Michael, it appears to have been a wonderful temporary gift meant just for that young woman.

Temporary charisms should be received with gratitude. Since they only manifest once or very rarely, you can't discern them. It is impossible to do much beyond praying, "Thank you, Lord! That was amazing!"

Charisms Are Not Natural Talents

The single biggest issue for a novice discerner is the critical distinction between charisms and your natural talents and abilities, or skills that you have learned. It's a very important issue because charisms are *not* natural talents, nor do natural talents somehow turn into charisms. In real life, we want to offer all that we are, to be used by God for his purposes, so we will often use our natural talents and spiritual gifts in the same setting. But for the purposes of discernment, we need to tease them apart and distinguish them.

The first thing to understand about charisms is that they cannot be inherited from our parents like many natural abilities are. For instance, I inherited some artistic ability from my father, while my brother is athletic and got through college on a basketball scholarship. But you receive your charisms sovereignly from the Holy Spirit, not from your parents through your chromosomes. Musical ability runs in the family of Father Michael Sweeney, and as a young man he was a skilled pianist.

But he insists he does not have a charism of Music. It's a natural talent that runs in his family, not a charism.

It is entirely possible that you could have been given a charism of Encouragement that God also gave to your mother. But you did not *inherit* the charism from your mother. God has sovereignly graced you both with the same gift because you both needed it for your particular call in life.

In real life, natural talents and charisms often work together. We are offering our whole selves to Jesus for his purposes. To be sure, we tease them apart and distinguish for the purposes of discernment. But if you see me teach, you will probably not be able to say, "*That* moment was the charism of Teaching at work, but she said *that* encouraging word because some teacher humiliated her in the fifth grade and she swore she would never do that to anyone else, and she picked up *that technique* in her teaching methodology course." In real life, it is all the same batch of dough being baked into the Eucharistic offering of our life on the altar.

A Charism Cannot Be Used for Evil

It is critical that we understand that a charism cannot be deliberately used for evil. You cannot run a drug-smuggling operation with a charism of Administration or use a charism of Writing to compose hate literature. The power of the Holy Spirit cannot be deliberately used for purposes contrary to the will of the Father. A charism empowers us to be an agent of God's mercy, love, beauty, truth, provision, and healing for others, bearing the kind of fruit for the Kingdom that is beyond our human abilities. There is only one purpose for these gifts: to serve the redemptive purposes of God and to remove obstacles to people encountering Christ. If someone deliberately attempts to use their charisms for evil, those charisms will wither away.

That said, we can sometimes inadvertently distort the exercise of our charisms by attempting to use them to meet our own needs. This can often happen early in the discernment process when we begin to realize we may have a particular charism. We may unconsciously try to get something we need from others (love/respect/material support/friendship, and so on) through the exercise of our charism. This is *not* the same thing as deliberately willing evil. It is more like striking an unspoken and often unconscious bargain: *I will exercise my charism for you and, in exchange, you will give me what I want.* We can try to manipulate things out of people through the exercise of our charisms. When we do so, our unresolved fears, anger, anxieties, or woundedness can seriously distort how our charism manifests.

For example, I knew a man that I will call "Ron" who had a genuine charism of Helps. The only problem was that Ron could not *not* help you. He would start helping his friend Phil, and at first, Phil would be very appreciative. But then, Phil would get used to being helped and stop giving as much positive feedback, and Ron would get restless. Ron was driven by a kind of unconscious "drug-seeking" behavior; the drug Ron was seeking endlessly was the affirmation of others. So he kept moving from helping relationship to helping relationship, in the constant search for a fresh supply of affirmation. As a result, he ended up with people half-helped everywhere. A mutual friend summed the dynamic up succinctly: "Underneath that compulsion is a charism somewhere."

If this scenario sounds all too familiar, it is okay. Almost all of us succumb to this temptation in the early phases of discernment. I certainly did. As you grow closer to God, though, your level of anxiety will diminish, your trust in God will grow, and you will find yourself freer to simply offer your gifts without strings attached, no payback required. The goal is a heart at rest in God that gives without expectation of reward, trusting the fruit of your gifts into God's hands, and leaving the others to respond in whatever way they choose.

This dynamic is one of the reasons the charisms have long been associated with saints. Their level of trust in God's love is so much higher that there is little distortion in the exercise of their charisms. They are wonderfully free to give their gifts without reservation and with no need to manipulate the apparent outcome. When that is true, God can do so much more through us!

If you become aware of this pattern in your own life, bring it to God and ask him to help you grow in your knowledge and trust in his love. Deliberately release the impact of your charisms in the lives of others to him and pray, "Lord, I trust you to meet my needs. In the meantime, I am going to seek to offer my gifts with no strings attached." Watch how he honors your trust and obedience.

How Many Charisms Can I Be Given?

While it is certainly possible that a man or woman might be given just a single charism, we have never actually met anybody with only a single charism (and we've taken more than 100,000 Catholics through this discernment process so far). People usually receive more than one gift but not fifteen (because they aren't the Body of Christ!). In our experience, individuals are typically given as few as two or as many as five charisms.

Charisms and the Disciplines of Discipleship

What is the relationship of charisms to the disciplines and actions that are fundamental to everyone who seeks to follow Jesus as his disciple in the midst of his Church? There are lots of things we do as Catholics (prayer, fasting, almsgiving, corporal and spiritual works of mercy, devotions, etc.) that are fundamental to our life as Catholics whether or not we have been given charisms in those specific areas.

So, for instance, one of the precepts of the Church is tithing. This is simple justice: the Church sees to our spiritual welfare, so it is only fair that we support the Church financially. We cannot just blow off our responsibility when they pass the plate at Mass, saying, "I don't have a charism of giving, so I'll let George over in the next pew do the heavy lifting because he does."

Nor are we off the hook when it comes to praying for others just because we do not have a charism of Intercessory Prayer. Praying for the living and the dead is one of the spiritual works of mercy to which all the baptized are called. Some of us are also given a charism in this area, which empowers us to pray for others with exceptional confidence and fruitfulness, but that does not mean that the rest of us are not supposed to pray or that God does not hear our prayers.

It is critical that we distinguish between those disciplines that are a normal part of the life of a Christian disciple and the presence of a supernatural empowerment in a specific area. This is particularly important because of our tendency to compare ourselves to somebody who has charisms that we do not have. It is tempting to judge ourselves because we do not see the same *kind* of fruit in our lives that another is bearing. But this is a great mistake.

We must not compare ourselves with others in that way. We are all called to bear witness to Christ to the best of our abilities, but perhaps we have a friend with a phenomenal charism of Evangelism who brings new people to RCIA every year. On the other hand, you might find that the reason people keep showing up at your door and leaving with a heart of gratitude for dinner and a good talk is that you've had a charism of Hospitality that you take for granted but which has healed and blessed more guests than you realize, something that your evangelist friend simply can't pull off.

As St. Paul wrote in Romans 12:4-8:

> For as in one body we have many parts, and all the parts do not have the same function, so we, though many, are one body in Christ and individually parts of one another. Since we have gifts that differ according to the grace given to us, let us exercise them: if prophecy, in proportion to the faith; if ministry, in ministering; if one is a teacher, in teaching; if one exhorts, in exhortation; if one contributes, in generosity; if one is over others, with diligence; if one does acts of mercy, with cheerfulness.

Now, let's dive into the fascinating nuts and bolts of the individual charisms.

CHAPTER 6

Pastoral and Communication Charisms

Instructing, advising, consoling, comforting, are spiritual works of mercy....

CATECHISM OF THE CATHOLIC CHURCH, 2447

In the Called & Gifted workshop, we look at twenty-three different charisms. To make it easier for participants to remember them all, we have divided the charisms into seven different groups according to their common focus.

SEVEN TYPES OF CHARISMS

- *Pastoral* charisms focus on the nurturing of people, whether as individuals or in community.
- *Communication* charisms focus on changing lives by communicating truth.
- *Organizational* charisms provide the structure, resources, and vision necessary to sustain a thriving organization or group.
- *Lifestyle* charisms fuel a distinctive lifestyle and freedom for unusual ministry.
- *Healing* charisms channel God's healing and restoration.
- *Understanding* charisms are directed toward understanding the ways of God, humanity, and creation.
- *Creative* charisms are expressed through creative activity that orders and beautifies.

Let's start with the Pastoral and Communication charisms.

PASTORAL CHARISMS:

Focus on the personal nurture of individuals and communities.

- Encouragement
- Helps
- Hospitality
- Mercy
- Pastoring

THE CHARISM OF ENCOURAGEMENT

Definition

Encouragement empowers a Christian to be an effective channel of God's love by strengthening and healing individuals in remarkable ways through his or her presence and words.

Description

Encouragement is the classic spiritual direction or counseling charism. Encouragers always focus on the individual. They never see a crowd; they see *you* in your uniqueness. Someone with this charism is used powerfully by the Holy Spirit to heal and build up individuals. They call forth and strengthen the unique person God has created you to be through their presence and their words. They see individuals through the eyes of God and encourage them to take their place in the Kingdom.

A Story of the Charism of Encouragement

St. Francis de Sales (1567-1622) was one of the seminal figures of a great revival in French Catholicism. As a newly ordained priest, Francis set out on foot to personally evangelize an entire area of Alpine France where the churches were in ruins and only one hundred practicing Catholics remained. Francis received over 40,000 people back into the Church and then was made bishop of the diocese that he had evangelized.

Francis had a charism of Encouragement and was a much-sought-after spiritual director. He understood that you did not have to be a priest or religious to become holy or live as a serious Christian disciple. His classic book, *Introduction to the Devout Life*, was the first major work on lay spirituality. Francis befriended and directed an extraordinarily wide circle of people: royalty, religious, clergy, lay men and women, and ordinary working people. This is very typical of someone with the charism of Encouragement. He saw the man or woman before him as God saw them, and by his words and presence he called them to walk more closely with Jesus Christ and to take their place in the Kingdom.

Applying This Charism

Those listening to a preacher or teacher with this charism will feel as if he or she is speaking to them personally — even in the midst of a crowd. Someone with this charism will prefer not to work primarily with large groups, but when working with a group they will still tune in to each individual member. They will be drawn to work or ministry that enables them to have extensive personal contact with individuals and will likely become frustrated if that is not possible.

I once had the fascinating experience of interviewing "George," who was a very effective teacher of elementary-age children. George was frustrated because he had not gotten a high score in Teaching and wanted to know what was wrong with this inventory! We were both surprised when we realized that *he was using the charism of Encouragement in a teaching setting.*

Here is a valuable rule of thumb: Different people can use different charisms fruitfully in the same job or setting. Indeed, how we go about the same job or ministry will vary widely depending on our charisms. So, one science teacher with a charism of Teaching may focus on empowering students who usually struggle with science to "get it." But a teacher in another classroom of first-graders may primarily be mentoring students individually through a gift of Encouragement. Both are effective but are exercising different gifts, and the primary impact they have on their students will therefore be different as well.

Evangelization and the Charism of Encouragement

This gift can be useful at all the thresholds of pre-discipleship as well as when working with maturing and discerning missionary disciples. The charism of Encouragement can be used fruitfully to help others at every stage of the spiritual journey.

Some Possible Expressions of Encouragement

- Counselor
- Spiritual director/confessor
- Mentor/coach
- Parent
- Teacher (especially of small children)
- Helping professional

THE CHARISM OF HELPS

Definition

The charism of Helps empowers a Christian to be a channel of God's goodness by using his or her skills, talents, and charisms to enable other individuals to serve God and people more fruitfully.

Description

Like Encouragement, the charism of Helps focuses on the individual. The people exercising this gift get their joy and satisfaction from assisting *you* to carry out the wonderful Kingdom mission to which God is calling you. Helpers know that the person they are assisting cannot successfully carry out the mission that God has given them without help. People with this gift tend to stand *behind* the person they are helping. People sometimes assume that "helpers" take this role because they are shy and retiring, but that is not necessarily true at all. In fact, those with the gift of helps serve the person they are assisting with formidable confidence.

I seem to evoke the charism of Helps in others. Several wonderful people over the years have taken one look at me and immediately recognized, "That woman needs help!" For instance, during the first break of the very first Called & Gifted workshop, a woman I had never met before walked up to me confidently and declared, "You are exactly the kind of personality I like least."

Her name was Lynn, and that first meeting was the unlikely beginning of a fruitful collaboration. She later told me that she already felt so drawn to helping me that she figured that the best defense was a strong offense. If she insulted me at the very beginning, she wouldn't have to get involved! The last word that anyone who knew her would use to describe Lynn was "shy." She had a gift-mix of Helps and Prophecy, which meant that she was a helper who was in your face.

Lynn became my greatest advocate, helper, and co-teacher over the next few years. She recruited people for workshops as well as helping set up and teach the workshops. Lynn told me early on, "Sherry, pack your bags. You're gonna be traveling." I was the Doubting Thomas. "Lynn, look around. There are *four* people in this room and that includes you and me! We are not on the fast track here." But Lynn was adamant. A million air miles later, it is clear that Lynn was a true prophet.

A Story of the Charism of Helps

Brother Leo (in fact, he was a priest) served as the closest disciple, secretary, and confessor of St. Francis of Assisi during the last years of the saint's life. (Brother Leo died c. 1270.) He was the only person present when Francis received the stigmata, and the only two documents we have in Francis' own hand were written to Brother Leo. He is an excellent example of someone with the gift of Helps, working behind the scenes to assist someone else who has a call from God that they cannot carry out on their own.

Applying This Charism

People with a charism of Helps are typically drawn to people with a charism of Leadership. It is common for disciples with a charism of Leadership and disciples with a charism of Helps to find one another. People with a charism of Helps need to see how what they are doing is making a real difference in the life of the person they are seeking to help or they will lose motivation.

Evangelization and the Charism of Helps

The evangelization focus of the charism of Helps is individuals. However, unlike Encouragement, this gift is directed more toward those who are emerging disciples and apostles. That's because the gift of Helps is all about assisting people who are trying to accomplish the mission for which God has anointed them, and people in the early thresholds are probably not yet ready to discern, much less answer, such a call. As a result, helpers will be most drawn to assist those in later thresholds of seeking and intentional discipleship as well as maturing disciples who are beginning to discern and live their personal vocation(s). Disciples with a charism of Helps will empower other evangelizers to bear abundant fruit.

Some Possible Expressions of Helps

- Support staff
- Ghost writer/editor
- Mentor/coach
- Supportive leader
- Teacher
- Parent

THE CHARISM OF HOSPITALITY

Definition

The charism of Hospitality empowers a Christian to be a generous channel of God's love by warmly welcoming and caring for those in need of food, shelter, and friendship.

Description

The charism of Hospitality is not about having a beautiful home or serving the best food (which might indicate a charism of Craftsmanship). Hospitality is about making a place for others as individuals and as a group. Someone with this charism may have to remove a stack of papers from a chair so you can sit down, but you will feel truly welcomed.

Hospitality is, along with the gift of Pastoring, one of the primary means by which God heals and strengthens individuals through the experience of Christian community. Someone with this gift has an amazing ability to create a warm, welcoming environment in which a person's needs for physical nurture, relational roots, and personal and spiritual companionship are met. Hospitality is a powerful ministry of healing.

A Story of the Charism of Hospitality

The gift of Hospitality is often thought of as "nice" but not powerful, as comforting but not transforming, and certainly not as evangelistic or prophetic. But like other charisms, Hospitality is an exercise of genuine spiritual power. St. Margaret Clitherow (born c. 1556) — a young wife, mother, and convert in sixteenth-century England — was martyred by the English state for exercising the charism of Hospitality.

In Margaret's day, it was illegal for an English man or woman to attend a Catholic Mass, to be reconciled with the Catholic Church, to go to confession, to be a priest or religious, or to knowingly offer hospitality to a priest or religious. Among the guests that Margaret warmly welcomed were Catholic priests who were risking their own lives so that lay Catholics might have access to the grace and consolation of the sacraments in the midst of persecution.

Margaret offered her home to be the primary "Mass center" in York; a place where Catholics could secretly gather to attend Mass and priests could be hidden as they passed through. Margaret had a secret room constructed upstairs in a house that adjoined her own, with a concealed passage running between the two homes. Visiting priests slept in the room and all Mass gear was stored there.

When safety permitted, Margaret delighted in feeding breakfast to all who had attended Mass in her home. She also offered space in her home to a Catholic schoolteacher to teach both her own children and a few of her neighbor's children. And she did all this knowing that should evidence of her priestly guests ever be discovered, she could receive the death penalty. In 1586, her home was searched and supplies for celebrating Mass were found. Margaret was tried and executed for her faith and daring hospitality.

Applying This Charism

People with the charism of Hospitality are very aware of the individual being welcomed. A person or family with this charism might welcome many individuals (as for instance, if somebody is running a bed and breakfast, or a shelter for the homeless). But they always see *you*. This charism can be exercised wherever people gather, including at work, in the community, and in the parish. Hospitality is a very valuable charism for building community in our large parishes.

Evangelization and the Charism of Hospitality

A disciple blessed with the gift of Hospitality can help people move through all stages of the journey from seeker to disciple to apostle. This charism has exceptional impact in pre-evangelization because the experience of empowered hospitality helps people cross into the early thresholds of trust, curiosity, and openness.

Some Possible Expressions of Hospitality

- Hospitality in your home, workplace, or parish
- Organizer of conferences/retreats
- Work with refugees/immigrants
- Work with homeless/abused women or children
- Facilitator of a small Christian community
- RCIA/Returning Catholics team member

THE CHARISM OF MERCY

Definition

The charism of Mercy empowers a Christian to be a channel of God's love through hands-on, practical deeds of compassion that relieve the distress of those who suffer and help them experience God's love.

Description

The heart of the charism of Mercy is hands-on, practical deeds that relieve suffering and restore dignity. The grace of the charism of Mercy addresses not just physical pain but also suffering. Suffering includes fear of the future, humiliation, anger, shame, loss of hope, abandonment, rejection, or despair. Those with a charism of Mercy not only alleviate physical suffering but also have an incredible ability to restore the dignity, hope, and sense of being loved by God to those who suffer.

Individuals with this gift find personally serving the poor, the rejected, and marginalized to be a compelling privilege even when it is difficult. Compassionate service of those who suffer lies at the heart of their spiritual life. They know in their bones that the words they will hear when they stand before God will be "Whatever you did for one of these least brothers of mine, you did for me" (Matthew 25:40).

I once worked with a nurse who told me, "It's very strange. I can just walk into a room where a patient is crawling the walls with fear, pain, or anxiety and they instantly calm down and relax into peace even though I haven't had time to do anything yet. I've noticed that this doesn't happen with all nurses." The difference was that, in addition to her training and skill, she was empowered by a charism of Mercy.

A Story of the Charism of Mercy

Venerable Henriette Delille (1812-1862) grew up in a world most of us know little about: Catholic antebellum New Orleans. The community was made up of three major groups: white slave-owners, black slaves, and in between, the *gens de couleur libres*, or "free people of color," like Henriette. Her family was racially mixed, educated, and French-speaking. *Gens de couleur libres* families often lived comfortable middle-class lives, but it came at a price.

Delille was also born into the *plaçage* system, a tradition in which Catholic women of mixed race became the mistresses of wealthy white Catholic men. In this tradition, it was acceptable for a white man to take a mixed-race mistress — who was known as a *placée* — when she was as young as twelve. When the white man reached marriageable age, he could choose to retain his *placée* and so have two families: his legal white family and his informal racially mixed family. The children of *placées* were often educated in France, as there were no schools available to educate mixed-race children in Louisiana, and it was illegal to teach blacks to read and write.

Henriette was raised to become a *placée*, as her mother, grandmother, and sister had been before her. These young women would attend the famous "Quadroon balls": lavish dances to which, beautifully dressed and carefully chaperoned, they would go to meet their future protectors. Men of color were only present at these balls as servants or musicians. The Church has discerned that Henriette's remarkable resistance to the racist culture in which she was raised was a sign of heroic virtue.

Henriette's turning point was meeting Sister St. Marthe Fontier, the first religious sister she had ever known. Sister St. Marthe had opened a Catholic school for young girls of color, and it became the nucleus for missionary activities. In order to secure more teachers to help her, Sister St. Marthe trained young girls like fourteen-year-old Henriette to become teachers.

Henriette's family was not happy with her new life (her mother had a nervous breakdown), especially because Henriette acknowledged her racial background and mixed with the black community. Because the women of her family had been *placées* for several generations, Henriette was what was then called an "octoroon": seven-eighths white and one-eighth black. Henriette's parents and brother listed themselves as "white" for the 1830 census because they could "pass," but Henriette chose to register as a "free person of color." Henriette would pay for that choice and for turning her back on a life of privilege.

Henriette could not join existing religious communities because they were open only to white women. Nonetheless,

Delille and two other *gens de couleur libres* women continued to pray together and teach non-whites. In 1836, they privately pledged themselves to God's service. They were not allowed to take formal vows for another ten years, when they became the Sisters of the Holy Family. The sisters served the black community with a home for the aged, schools, and orphanages. The sisters were so poor in the early days that sometimes all they had for dinner was sweetened water.

Exhausted by overwork and a long illness, Henriette died in 1862, the year that the Union Army took New Orleans, and she never saw the end of slavery. Her obituary summed up her life this way: "For the love of Jesus Christ, she made herself the humble and devoted servant of the slaves."[1] Like St. Teresa of Kolkata, disciples with this charism are powerful witnesses, because their lives do not make sense if God does not exist.

Applying This Charism

Someone with the charism of Mercy could be the mechanic who fixes used cars for single moms, a pillar of the St. Vincent de Paul ministry or the food pantry, or the one who provides a weekly hot meal for the hungry. Medical professionals and workers or volunteers in hospices, refugee camps, or prisons may also be working out of a charism of Mercy.

I have had to sometimes remind organizers of initiatives for the poor, who have the charism of Mercy, that their spiritual life will falter if they don't also have a chance to work directly with those who suffer. Administration is not a substitute for direct hands-on service for people with this gift. For those who have been given this charism, direct service to those who suffer is a

---

[1] Sisters of the Holy Family website (online at http://www.sistersofthe holyfamily.com/AboutHenrietteDelillereview.html, as of May 5, 2017).

major form of prayer. It can be very damaging to their spiritual lives to let other pressures keep them from hands-on participation for too long.

Evangelization and the Charism of Mercy

Mercy is a powerful charism of witness that can have a big pre-evangelization impact, both in the wider culture and on the lives of individuals and families. The exercise of the charism of Mercy can be very important in evangelization because it fosters spiritual trust and rouses intense curiosity in the skeptical nonbeliever.

Some Possible Expressions of Mercy

- Medical professional
- Social worker
- Hospice worker
- Hospital or prison chaplain or volunteer
- St. Vincent de Paul Society volunteer
- Volunteer chore services worker

THE CHARISM OF PASTORING

Definition

The charism of Pastoring empowers a Christian to be an effective channel of God's love, building Christian community by nurturing the relationships and long-term spiritual growth of a group.

Description

First of all, the *charism* of Pastoring is not the same as the *office* of a Catholic pastor of a parish, which requires ordination. The charism can be given to priests or laypeople, men or women. The gift is directed toward shepherding groups, not individuals. Also notable is that the people with this charism function primarily *within* the Christian community rather than outside it because Pastoring is about building the Christian community.

Someone with the charism of Pastoring eagerly seeks to promote the long-term spiritual growth of individuals in and through Christian community. People with the gift of Pastoring nurture the network of relationships between believing Christians by bringing them together to pray, study, or share their faith so that they will mature and bear much fruit. Gathering people into groups to grow is their methodology. If your parish doesn't already have small Christian communities, someone with this gift will be eager to start them! I knew a couple who seemed to share this charism, and together they started and led their parish's flourishing married couples' groups.

A Story of the Charism of Pastoring

Henry Michael Buch (d. 1666) was part of the same great seventeenth-century French revival as St. Francis de Sales. He was the son of poor day laborers who had been effectively evangelizing and discipling many of his fellow shoemakers for years. Henry eventually founded a confraternity of shoemakers and tailors, the Frères Cordonniers ("Brother Shoemakers"). Members of the confraternity would approach their trade as disciples and apostles, evangelize their co-workers, share their earnings with the poor, and live a common spiritual life according to an informal rule. The confraternity eventually spread around France and Italy.

Henry pastored other laymen: evangelizing his fellow shoemakers, bringing them together in Christian community, and helping them grow as disciples and apostles. *Apostolicam Actuositatem* (Decree on the Apostolate of the Laity) seems to be describing Henry and so many other lay leaders in our large parishes who are personally engaged in fostering community and making disciples:

> The laity with the right apostolic attitude supply what is lacking to their brethren and refresh the spirit of pastors and of the rest of the faithful (cf. 1 Cor 16:17-18).... They bring to the Church people who perhaps are far removed from it, earnestly cooperate in presenting the word of God especially by means of catechetical instruction, and offer their special skills to make the care of souls ... more efficient and effective.[2]

Applying This Charism

The United States is filled with large parishes. Institute teachers have worked in parishes that are the size of small cities with twenty thousand or thirty thousand members. The charism of Pastoring is an important part of God's provision for our situation because a single priest cannot possibly manage care of the souls of three thousand people by himself.

Pastoring is one of the few charisms directed overwhelmingly toward people within the Church. You might be running a Bible study or faith-sharing or prayer group in your workplace, home, or a local coffee shop, but the purpose of the group will be on

---

[2] *Apostolicam Actuositatem*, 10, 24; Pope St. John Paul II, *Christifideles Laici*, 33.

strengthening the Christian community. A man or woman with this charism prefers to work with groups that are small enough to know everyone in the group personally: twenty people, not two hundred. People enjoy being part of small groups facilitated by someone with the charism of Pastoring because the group experience is rich, encouraging, and often life-changing.

Evangelization and the Charism of Pastoring

In terms of initial conversion, a leader with the charism of Pastoring can be very helpful to those who have reached the threshold of seeking and are on the cusp of intentional discipleship. Individuals with this gift are most effective working with people in later stages of spiritual development: seeking, intentional disciple, and apostle.

Some Possible Expressions of Pastoring

- Pastor of a small parish
- Pastoral staff member
- Prayer-group leader
- Bible-study leader
- Facilitator of a small Christian community
- RCIA team member (especially focused on the catechumenate and mystagogia)

COMMUNICATION CHARISMS:
Focus on transforming lives through communicating truth.

- Evangelism
- Prophecy
- Teaching

THE CHARISM OF EVANGELISM

Definition

The charism of Evangelism empowers a Christian to be an effective channel of God's love by sharing the faith with others — baptized or not — in a way that draws them to intentionally follow Jesus as his disciple in the midst of his Church.

Description

Those given the gift of Evangelism seek to bring those who do not know Jesus to an encounter with him and to help those who do not know him well to become his disciples in the center of his Church. They are constantly asking, "Where are these individuals in their living relationship with God, and how can I help them move closer to Jesus and his Church?" In the presence of someone with this charism, even unbelievers and skeptics can find talking about God with the evangelizer to be intriguing and compelling.

Consequently, most people with this gift are not much interested in insider ecclesial debates. They are too busy looking for ways to start spiritual conversations with friends — at work, at the gym, or over coffee or a couple of beers.

Stories of the Charism of Evangelism

David VanVickle is a parish director of evangelization. He regaled members of our Forming Intentional Disciples Facebook Forum with wonderful stories of his experience during Pope Francis' visit to the United States. Dave stood in line for four hours to get into the Washington, D.C., papal Mass and described it as an "evangelizer's paradise." Dave found himself surrounded by a sea of intrigued non-believers. All he had to do to start a spiritual conversation was to ask people why they were there. A skeptical woman told him that she was there because she was passionate about the environment and she wanted to see the pope who had written about it. One man, sporting a Mohawk, told Dave that he had come to see if Pope Francis was right about "that Jesus guy." Dave prayed with that man on the spot.

Dave prays that God will give him a "divine appointment" every day: "If you send someone to me and make it obvious, I'll share about you with them." As stunning as the following story may sound, experiences like this are actually fairly common for those given a charism of Evangelism. It is a pattern we have heard described in interviews for years: either searching people can somehow sense our charisms or the Holy Spirit inspires them to approach us and ask us for what we have been given to give.

Dave was waiting for a flight in a U.S. airport and was reading his Bible when a large Muslim family came and sat close to him. One young man kept looking at his Bible. Dave tried to smile at him, but he quickly looked away. Dave finally decided to visit the restroom before it was time to board.

Dave was in a stall when he heard someone enter the stall next to him. Then he heard a man speaking in very broken English: "Excuse me ... were you the man reading in the gate?" Immediately, Dave realized it was the young Muslim man he had noticed at his gate. Dave thought maybe he had left something behind so he answered, "Yes." The young man spoke softly, "Can you tell me about Jesus?" Dave responded, "Sure, let's grab some coffee." His new acquaintance spoke even more softly, "No! My father cannot know about this."

So, for the next twenty minutes, Dave quietly talked to this man about Jesus through the partition. Dave could hear the man crying through the partition when he spoke of how Jesus loved him unconditionally. Then Dave told his friend that "Jesus is ready to come into your heart right now, and we can pray and invite him in." They prayed and after they were done, Dave heard the young man say softly, "I knew you were more than a dream."

The man explained to Dave that he had grown up in a part of the world that was so completely Muslim he had only heard Quranic references to Jesus. But the young man reported that every night for a month, he had had a dream of a man named Jesus who was hanging, bloodied, on a cross. The man on the cross in his dream looked at him and said, "I love you."

Dave slipped his Bible under the partition and the man quickly hid it in his bag and left. Dave never saw his face.[3]

Applying This Charism

The gift of Evangelism can be exercised in a giant gathering like World Youth Day or with one person in intimate conversation. The goal is the same: to give everyone a chance to respond to what Jesus has accomplished for us and the universal call to follow him.

Evangelization and the Charism of Evangelism

Why do I call the charism Evangelism instead of evangelization? Simple. I needed to distinguish the charism from the larger mission. Evangelization is the entire primary mission of the Church and includes everything involved in helping human beings reach heaven (the care of souls) as well as the Kingdom

---

[3] Dave VanVickle, private correspondence, February 10, 2017.

transformation of human cultures and structures. *All* individual charisms contribute to the Church's primary mission of evangelization in different ways. The charism of Evangelism is far more narrow than the mission of evangelization and zeroes in on one specific part of that overall mission.

People with the gift of Evangelism usually focus intensely on pre-evangelization and initial proclamation of Christ, where they get to share the Great Story of Jesus. This charism is particularly helpful when helping those at thresholds of curiosity, openness, and seeking, and it can greatly aid those who are struggling with the choice to "drop their nets" and become intentional disciples.

Some Possible Expressions of Evangelism

- RCIA team member
- Returning Catholics program team member
- Preacher
- Apologist
- Writer/blogger
- Missionary

THE CHARISM OF PROPHECY

Definition

The charism of Prophecy empowers a Christian to be a channel of divine truth and wisdom by communicating a word or call of God to individuals or a group through inspired words or actions.

Description

God is no longer adding to the deposit of faith (which includes both Scripture and Tradition), but God is still speaking to his Church (CCC 79). This does not mean that any given private prophecy is infallibly true (its divine origin and truthfulness must be discerned in light of revelation), or that its meaning will be obvious (it often is not and can take a long time to understand), or that it will be concerned with predicting the future (it usually is not).

The charism of Prophecy can take many forms, including a prophetic exhortation that calls people to action; a "word of knowledge" or "word of wisdom" through which God reveals what he is doing (such as a healing) in the life of an individual or community; an interior vision (not an apparition) or prophetic actions through which God's word to a community is communicated.

Stories of the Charism of Prophecy

Deacon Keith Strohm tells this story:

> I was talking with a woman who had endured a difficult life and had had multiple abortions. She was struggling to believe that there was a God who loved her and who even cared about her pain.
>
> As she talked, I kept hearing a name over and over again in my head. I was conflicted as to whether this was from God or had anything to do with her story. Finally, I asked her what this name has to do with her story. She broke down and began to cry. She had been to a retreat for post-abortive women where they encouraged her to

name the child or children that were aborted. The name I had shared with her was the name that she had given one of the children she had aborted ... and she hadn't told a single person, not even her husband. This woman needed to know that God saw her pain.[4]

Receiving a prophetic word was a major turning point for Katherine Coolidge, who was raised as a Baptist but now serves as the Institute's Called & Gifted coordinator:

I actually received a word from a Baptist minister when I was wrestling with becoming Catholic. It meant giving up the idea of becoming a missionary. He said to me: "I shouldn't be saying this — if anyone ever finds out, I will be defrocked — but I need to tell you that you will be a missionary ... just not in the Baptist missions but in the Catholic Church."

I was stunned. As I pondered his words, it was as if all I knew about Catholic teaching and Scripture just began to align. Not with any earthly idea how it would come to pass but just an assurance I was truly being sent into the Church.

That was Monday. I called the priest who was preparing me that evening. Immediately, he asked me to meet him at the church on Wednesday so I could be received that day. He told me later he felt as if those words came from the Lord himself, and it was clear to him what he was to do.[5]

---

[4] Deacon Keith Strohm, private correspondence, February 13, 2017.
[5] Katherine Coolidge, private correspondence, February 13, 2017.

Applying This Charism

Any genuine prophetic word will not be in opposition to, and must always be discerned in light of Scripture, Tradition, and the Magisterium. Ongoing pastoral discernment and oversight is essential so that the community can fully benefit from this charism.

Most people exercising this charism are quite ordinary people who know that it is vital that God's people respond to his call today with their whole hearts. A good deal of emotional and spiritual maturity and disinterested discipline is necessary for someone with this charism to exercise it fruitfully. It is both possible and somewhat common in practice to unintentionally offer our own ideas or concerns in whole or part as a prophetic word. Disciples used by God in this way must communicate the message they have been given and leave the results to God and to the discernment of the individual or Christian community.

Evangelization and the Charism of Prophecy

Evangelizers are sometimes given words of knowledge or wisdom for someone else that moves them into spiritual curiosity or openness very quickly. The charism of Prophecy can be particularly helpful for those at the thresholds of curiosity, openness, and seeking.

Some Possible Expressions of Prophecy

- Prayer-group member
- Healing-prayer team member
- Confessor

- Social-justice activist
- Writer
- Influential religious or moral figure

THE CHARISM OF TEACHING

Definition

Teaching empowers a Christian to be a channel of God's truth and wisdom by enabling others to learn information and skills that help them reach their fullest spiritual and personal potential.

Description

People with the charism of Teaching are all about empowering others to learn information or skills because it will change their lives. These people live for the joy of witnessing the great "Aha!" moment when the learner they are working with grasps the implications of some new knowledge or skill. The information or skill being taught can be either religious or secular, and the charism can be used to teach either individuals or groups.

In the presence of this gift, people who normally do not like a subject nor do well in it suddenly find it surprisingly interesting. Those with the charism are attentive to two things: (1) the content they want to teach and (2) the person who needs to learn it and how best to get that content across to them. Teachers often find themselves making lesson plans in their heads as soon as they have learned something new themselves. They are always thinking how they can pass on their knowledge or skills to others. People with the charism of teaching are confident that wonderful fruit will be borne from the learning that has taken place.

A Story of the Charism of Teaching

St. Jean-Baptiste de la Salle lived in France from 1651 to 1719, a couple of generations after St. Francis de Sales and the "generation of saints." Jean was already ordained when he met a layman who had a vision for starting a school for poor boys (in an era when public education did not yet exist). Jean became involved with the school and finally gathered a nucleus of lay teachers about him to whom he taught a new way of educating children.

This group became the Christian Brothers, the first men's religious community devoted entirely to offering free education to the poor. To focus entirely on the teaching vocation, Jean laid down the rule that no brother could become a priest. Jean's system of education — teaching many children simultaneously and in the local colloquial dialect, rather than the language of the elite (which enabled the students to share what they were learning with their parents) — revolutionized elementary education. He persisted in the face of great resistance to the idea of an educated working class. Evangelization and spiritual formation was integrated into the heart of De la Salle's educational vision.

Applying This Charism

The charism of Teaching is valuable in the evangelization of both individuals and groups as well as playing a major role in the pre-evangelization of culture. The Catholic school system was founded in response to the challenge of the Reformation to form a new kind of lay Catholics who could pass their faith on to their children and explain and defend their faith to their non-Catholic friends and neighbors. The charism of Evangelism is also an essential part of the DNA of Catholic schools. Many with this charism prefer to work in Catholic schools because of the freedom they have to speak openly about God there.

Evangelization and the Charism of Teaching

The charism of Teaching is especially helpful with the work of initiatory catechesis and to people at thresholds of seeking and intentional discipleship as well as for emerging apostles.

Some Possible Expressions of Teaching

- Public school/adult education teacher
- Religious education
- Tutor/volunteer teacher
- Creator of educational curriculum
- Leader of educational organization
- Home-schooling parent

CHAPTER SEVEN

Organizational and Lifestyle Charisms

My personal definition of voluntary poverty is the sincere will to do without as much as one can in order to be free to live a full human life.

WILLIAM GAUCHAT[1]

ORGANIZATIONAL CHARISMS:
Meeting the vision or structural needs of an organization or group.

- Administration
- Leadership
- Giving
- Service

THE CHARISM OF ADMINISTRATION

Definition

The charism of Administration empowers a Christian to be an effective channel of God's wisdom through planning and dele-

---

[1] Quoted from *The Dorothy Day Book: A Selection From Her Writings and Readings*, Margaret Quigley and Michael Garvey, eds. (Springfield, IL: Templegate Publishers, 1982), p. 89.

gation, and by coordinating the resources and efforts of a group to accomplish a Kingdom purpose.

Description

The sign of a charism of Administration is not having a tidy sock drawer. People with this charism love to *lead a group to achieve a complicated task*. They don't necessarily come up with the original vision, but they are really effective at leading a group to implement the vision by planning, delegating, and then coordinating the efforts of a group.

Delegation is their particular forte because they prefer to make things happen through the efforts of others. They can break up a complicated task and delegate different responsibilities to a number of different people while coordinating the efforts of the whole group. They are "make it happen" people who are especially energized and fruitful when asked to lead a group to *make it happen*.

A Story of the Charism of Administration

St. Louise de Marillac (1591-1660), the daughter of a French nobleman, received an excellent education. Already a widow when she met St. Vincent de Paul, Louise eventually became involved with his Confraternities of Charity.

In 1634, Louise and St. Vincent de Paul founded the Daughters of Charity, a religious community of working-class women whom Louise trained to care for the sick and the poor in systematic ways. At first, the Daughters served the needs of the sick and the poor in their homes. However, Louise was a gifted administrator and developed a system of pastoral care that her sisters carried out in the largest hospital in Paris.

Their work in Paris was so well regarded that the Daughters were invited to take over management of the nursing services of another hospital in the west of France. There, Louise pioneered a highly successful team approach among the doctors, nurses, and other hospital staff, which the community still uses today. Eventually, the efforts of the Daughters expanded to encompass orphanages; to people who were elderly, mentally ill, or imprisoned; and even to the battlefield.

Applying This Charism

People like working with someone with a charism of Administration because they know it will be a positive, low-stress experience: their time will not be wasted, their responsibilities will be clear, and the mission will be accomplished. Disciple-administrators are some of the most effective people-helpers because most of God's provision reaches us through the organizations or institutions that disciples with this charism are empowered to build and sustain.

Evangelization and the Charism of Administration

Disciples with the charism of Administration are critical to organizing effective and fruitful hospitality, evangelization, and outreach initiatives that enable the Christian community to offer multiple opportunities for others to encounter Jesus in the midst of his Church. Administrators are essential to implementing an evangelizing vision and creating and sustaining a missional "trellis" that supports a parish culture of fruit-bearing discipleship.

Some Possible Expressions of Administration

- Executive/administrator
- Office manager
- Parish administrator
- Parish or finance council member
- Committee head
- Community or parish organizer

THE CHARISM OF LEADERSHIP

Definition

The charism of Leadership empowers a Christian to be an agent of God's purposes by sharing a new and compelling vision of a better future with others and then directing the overall efforts of the group as they work together to make that vision a reality.

Description

People with a charism of Leadership contemplate the world about them, asking, "What can we do together to change things for the better?" When a disciple with this gift conceives and shares a vision, many find it so compelling that they want to join the effort to make the vision a reality. Disciples with this gift typically found new vision-centered groups or organizations.

One fundamental test for whether or not you have a charism of Leadership is this: When you run a new vision up the flagpole, do people find it intriguing and salute?

A Story of the Charism of Leadership

St. Ignatius of Loyola (1491-1556) was born into a noble family in Spain. His military career was cut short by a cannon ball that seriously damaged his knee at age thirty-one. While confined to bed, he experienced a dramatic conversion as he read the lives of the saints. Ignatius eventually gathered a group of six men who would become the first Jesuits, and he led them through his life-changing Spiritual Exercises. He was fifty when he became the first superior general of a new men's religious community, the Society of Jesus.

A wonderful leader of men, Ignatius spent the rest of his life in Rome, directing the complex missionary initiatives of his far-flung order. Under Ignatius' leadership, the community grew rapidly. When he died fifteen years later, there were over one thousand Jesuits.

Applying This Charism

People often confuse the charisms of Leadership and Administration because they are both group-oriented gifts. The difference is that those with a charism of Leadership will come up with the original vision and gather a new group about that vision, while someone with the gift of Administration wants to coordinate a group's efforts to implement an existing vision. Disciples given the gift of Leadership need people with the charism of Administration about them.

There are two questions I always ask someone who is discerning a possible charism of Leadership: (1) Have you ever started a new mission-centered group or organization? (2) Has someone with a charism of Helps offered to help you carry out a vision? I ask this second question because people with a charism of Helps are regularly drawn to leaders with a vision they cannot accomplish on their own.

Evangelization and the Charism of Leadership

Disciples with the charism of Leadership can be useful starting and leading a wide variety of group initiatives focusing on pre-evangelization, initial proclamation, and initiatory catechesis. They are also effective at calling forth emerging missional leaders.

Some Possible Expressions of Leadership

- Pastor of mission-centered parish
- Founder of a new movement, organization, or mission-centered group
- Creative head/re-founder of an organization, group, or business
- Innovator whose ideas spawn new missional groups
- Small-group mission leader
- Vision-casting teacher/preacher

THE CHARISM OF GIVING

Definition

The charism of Giving empowers a Christian to be a cheerful channel of God's provision by giving money and material goods with extraordinary generosity to those in need.

Description

This charism is not about simply giving of yourself. It is centered around giving financial and/or material resources (money, food, clothing, property, etc.) so that the needs of others are met and the purposes of God can be achieved. Disciples with the charism of giving either are empowered to make money or find that money and other resources mysteriously come to them so that these things can be provided to others.

Stories of the Charism of Giving

For ten years, St. Vincent de Paul personally took on the financial relief of the Duchy of Lorraine, which was devastated by famine and war. He raised and sent the equivalent of $97 million to the region via an astonishing member of his religious community: Brother Mathieu Regnard (1592-1669).

Brother Mathieu made fifty, 450-mile round trips to Lorraine, bearing large amounts of cash, while successfully eluding bands of robbers and pillaging armies. He would always return to Paris from each trip with as many desperate people as possible — a hundred at a time. The refugees would receive welcome and care at Vincent de Paul's headquarters. People were amazed at Monsignor Vincent's extraordinary efforts because Lorraine was a foreign country rather than part of France at the time.[2]

I once met a widow, "Edith," who was nearing retirement age. She told me that she had gone through a conversion two years previously. By the time I met her, Edith was having the time of her life, giving thousands of dollars away. She laughed,

---

[2] Bernard Pujo, *Vincent de Paul: The Trailblazer* (Notre Dame, IN: University of Notre Dame Press, 2004), p. 132.

"If my children had any idea how much I am giving away, they would have me locked up!"

But what most surprised Edith was the discovery that, in her words, "I literally cannot *out-give* God! As soon as I give money away, it keeps coming back to me in the most unexpected ways. The government has contacted me twice to tell me that *they* owe *me* money. Who ever heard of anything like this?"

Applying This Charism

To exercise this charism, you do not have to be wealthy. But what all disciples with this gift have in common is that they are consistently used by God as a channel through which provision flows to individuals, families, groups, or organizations. They are confident that their own material needs will be met by God; meanwhile they delight in meeting the needs of others and of the Kingdom.

Evangelization and the Charism of Giving

The charism of Giving can transform a family, an institution, or a whole region, but it is also powerfully directed at individuals. People who struggle with belief in God's love and care can have their entire spiritual worldview transformed by witnessing or being the recipients of dramatic acts of generosity. Witnessing this charism in action can be enormously thought-provoking for agnostics and atheists as well as those at any threshold of pre-discipleship. It can also greatly strengthen the faith of disciples and apostles in need.

Some Possible Expressions of Giving

- Fund-raiser
- Board member of a charitable organization

- Exceptionally generous giver
- Visionary philanthropist
- Leader in stewardship/philanthropic circles
- Creative worker for economic justice/solidarity

THE CHARISM OF SERVICE

Definition

Service empowers a Christian to be a channel of God's purposes by recognizing the gaps or unmet needs that prevent good things from happening, and by personally doing whatever it takes to bridge the gap or meet the need.

Description

This is one of the most common and least appreciated of all the charisms. People with a charism of Service have a kind of radar for the unmet needs around them and are personally motivated to respond in a hands-on way to meet those needs. People with this charism are motivated to fill vacuums that prevent good things from happening. They are typically self-starting and multi-talented, a jack-of-all-trades.

A Story of the Charism of Service

Blessed Catherine Jarrige (1754-1836) was born into a peasant farming family in France and became a Third Order Dominican at age twenty-two. During the French Revolution, religious orders were suppressed, and priests and nuns were imprisoned and murdered. The Church was driven underground.

Fearless and ingenious, Catherine set up a clandestine network to aid hunted priests. Exhibiting the practical creativity characteristic of Service, she hid them in robbers' dens and provided them with vestments, Mass supplies, food, shelter, safe passage, and false papers — risking her life multiple times. In her region, no babies went unbaptized and no one died without last rites. She lost only one priest, Servant of God François Filiol, and she accompanied him to the guillotine. After his execution, she took some of his blood and smeared it on the face of a blind child whose sight was restored. The executioner saw this and began to cry: "I'm lost. I'm lost. I've killed a saint!" Catherine was arrested several times but always released because of her popularity with the local people.

One of Catherine's most remarkable adventures was getting two hidden priests past a local revolutionary leader. She dressed them like peasants, doused them with liquor, and told them to stagger like they were drunk and let her do the talking. They met the revolutionary on the road. To distract him, Catherine screamed at him like a fishwife. The revolutionary confided to the nearest priest-in-disguise, "Citizen, if I had a wife like that, I would take her to the nearest river and drown her." Catherine successfully hid those priests for two years.[3]

After the Revolution, Catherine helped restart local parish life and the local hospital. She was also known for her constant begging for and care of the poor. Her whole life was serving God and his people by tackling any need she saw in front of her with creativity, energy, and love.

Applying This Charism

It is important to understand that the charism of Service is not a charism of Administration. Disciples with the gift of

---

[3] Sister Mary Jean Dorcy, O.P., *Saint Dominic's Family: Over 300 Famous Dominicans* (Rockford, IL: TAN Books, 1983), p. 494.

Service are motived by the presence of vacuums and unfilled organizational gaps that stop good things from happening. *They do not want to delegate*; they make things happen by taking personal, hands-on action.

However, because they are so capable and proactive, they are often moved quickly into leadership in voluntary organizations. As a result, people with a charism of Service can become over-committed in all the wrong places. As one young woman with a charism of Service complained to me: "They put me on the parish council. I *loathe* the parish council! I don't want to sit around talking about things. *I want to do it myself!*"

Curiously, because they are so good at anticipating needs and filling them before the rest of us get around to it, disciples with this charism can sometimes experience a backlash. People around them can feel that they are showing off or making other people look lazy or incompetent. The truth is that when somebody else who can do the job better shows up, people exercising a charism of Service will easily step aside and go find another organizational gap to fill. The challenge for someone with this charism is discerning when and where to say "no."

Evangelization and the Charism of Service

Seeing somebody continually pouring themselves out in acts of service for neighbors, groups, and the community can be powerfully moving for unbelievers and the skeptical. Witnessing the charism of Service in action often builds trust, rouses spiritual curiosity, and fosters openness to the possibility of spiritual and personal change.

Some Possible Expressions of Service

- Exceptional volunteer
- Community/parish activist
- Handyman/woman
- Support staff/administrative assistant
- Troubleshooter
- Critical committee member

LIFESTYLE CHARISMS:
Empower a distinctive lifestyle and freedom for unusual ministry.

- Celibacy
- Faith
- Missionary
- Voluntary Poverty

Lifestyle charisms can sound pretty straightforward, but their discernment is rather complex. You can't realize, "Hey, I was celibate for two hours last week and it went great!" and draw the conclusion that you obviously have the charism of Celibacy — just as you can't determine that you have a gift of Missionary by spending a couple of hours with someone from another culture.

The Lifestyle charisms, by their very nature, cannot be discerned in a few hours a week because it is a call to a *lifestyle*. To discern these gifts, you need to ponder and pray through recurring patterns in your past as well as explore the possibility of these charisms in the present. Typically, Lifestyle charisms take longer to discern than other gifts.

THE CHARISM OF CELIBACY

Definition

Celibacy empowers a Christian to be most fulfilled and spiritually fruitful by remaining unmarried and celibate for the sake of Christ.

Description

For someone with this gift, a celibate life is *not* a void; it is not just the absence of marriage or romantic attachment. It is a *positive* call to a particular relational lifestyle that carries with it the freedom to take on unusual vocations or missions. Friendship is the primary kind of relational intimacy to which those with this gift are called. Friendship is a kind of real intimacy, but it is not exclusive. Friendship is not a vocation to the exclusive, sexual intimacy of marriage.

The charism of Celibacy is not just given to priests and religious but also to lay men and women. In our culture, it can be very difficult to view celibacy as a positive call and gift of God. I have met young adults who were both puzzled and perturbed when they instinctively backed away as a cherished friendship started to turn romantic. When a disciple seeking God's will for his or her life discovers that he or she may have a charism of Celibacy, it opens the door to all kinds of new possibilities — some religious and some secular. For instance, becoming a consecrated virgin while continuing to live a secular life is a formally recognized ecclesial vocation that is re-emerging as a possibility for women.

Catholics sometimes suppose that those with a charism of Celibacy cannot be tempted sexually, but that is not true.

Nevertheless, their ultimate fruitfulness and fulfillment comes through remaining unmarried and chaste and therefore free to be totally dedicated to the mission for which God has called and gifted them.

A Story of the Charism of Celibacy

St. Kateri Tekakwitha (1656-1680) was an Algonquin-Mohawk woman living in what is now upstate New York and southern Canada. Her Algonquin mother, a Christian convert from a largely non-Christian tribe, had been taken prisoner by the Mohawks. She married a Mohawk man to whom she bore Kateri. When all the members of her immediate family died of smallpox, four-year-old Kateri became a member of her uncle's family.

Kateri instinctively resisted the Mohawk tradition of early marriage and was finally able to declare her desire to be baptized. She was already spiritually quite advanced when she was baptized by a Jesuit missionary at nineteen and given the Christian name "Kateri," after St. Catherine of Siena. In her Mohawk community, she was called the "Christian" and increasingly persecuted for her faith. Kateri was able to escape to a remarkably devout Catholic village made up of converts from many different tribes in southern Canada. Here, Kateri was quickly recognized and honored as a mystic, ascetic, and living saint by the people of the village.

Despite her obvious devotion and holiness, the French missionaries who worked among the Mohawks were very hesitant to let Kateri make a vow of Celibacy because it was so contrary to Mohawk culture. Kateri's response was recorded by a priest who knew her:

I have deliberated enough. For a long time, my decision on what I will do has been made. I have consecrated myself entirely to Jesus, son of Mary, I have chosen Him for husband and He alone will take me for wife.[4]

Kateri became the first Native American consecrated virgin in 1679. Kateri had been badly scarred by smallpox as a child. Yet those who were with her when she died the next year at age twenty-four reported that, shortly after she died, her scars vanished and her skin became clear and radiant.

Word spread quickly, "The saint is dead." Hundreds came to pray before Kateri's grave. Many miracles of physical healing were reported at her grave and when sick people were touched by a piece of her clothing. Within a few months, Kateri was being called "Protectress of Canada" by the local faithful. She was canonized by Pope Benedict XVI in 2012.

Applying This Charism

It is important for those with a charism of Celibacy to seriously contemplate the other charisms they have been given. Celibacy gives one freedom for something else, and that something else will be significantly shaped and colored by one's other charisms.

Evangelization and the Charism of Celibacy

The expression of the charism of Celibacy will likely impact those who are in the later stages of the journey: namely, disciples and emerging apostles who are grappling with the question, "Where is God calling me?" Celibates can bear potent witness here because they witness to the possibility of a joyful, fulfilling

---

[4] K. I. Koppedrayer, "The Making of the First Iroquois Virgin: Early Jesuit Biographies of the Blessed Kateri Tekakwitha," *Ethnohistory* (Durham, NC: Duke University), Vol. 40, No. 2. (Spring 1993), pp. 277-306.

life that is completely dedicated to Christ. The charism of Celibacy calls us to live a life that would not make sense if God did not exist.

Some Possible Expressions of Celibacy

- Priesthood
- Religious sister or brother
- Consecrated virgin
- Lay missionary
- Work with the poor
- Ministry to single adults

THE CHARISM OF EXTRAORDINARY FAITH

Definition

The charism of Extraordinary Faith empowers a Christian to be an effective agent of God's purposes through a radical trust in the love, power, and provision of God and an extraordinary freedom to act on that trust.

Description

St. Thomas Aquinas clearly distinguished between the *charism* of "Faith" (which we named "Extraordinary Faith," to make the distinction clear) and the *virtue* of faith, which is necessary for salvation.[5] The charism is quite rare, while the theological virtue is given to all the baptized.

---

[5] St. Thomas Aquinas, *Summa Theologiae*, I-II, q111, a4, ad2 (online at http://www.newadvent.org/summa/2111.htm, as of May 5, 2017).

When helping someone discern the charism of Extraordinary Faith, one of the first things we look for is a pattern of risk-taking for God's purposes. Such a pattern might look like Mother Teresa believing that God will provide for all the needs of her sisters and the poor they serve without raising money. Or like the Catholic man I met years ago who had once smuggled Bibles into the former Soviet Union. When the rest of his team were waiting in great anxiety for the secret police to pounce, he was having the time of his life and couldn't understand why the rest of his group was so nervous!

For those with the charism, this kind of risk-taking is not recklessness or carelessness. Unless you have been given a charism of Extraordinary Faith, it is perfectly appropriate to go about your mission in more conventional ways. But those given this particular charism feel free to color outside the lines, because in their experience God always makes a way and often that way is remarkable.

Disciples with this charism don't need to know where the money necessary for a project that God is calling them to is going to come from or know in advance exactly how their initiative is going to work out. Where the average Christian sees a wall, the person of Extraordinary Faith sees an open door. The person with the charism of Extraordinary Faith often feels a spontaneous rush of confidence in God in the midst of an impossible situation.

A Story of the Charism of Extraordinary Faith

St. Frances Xavier Cabrini (1850-1917) had a wonderful charism of Extraordinary Faith. Cabrini founded sixty-seven institutions during her lifetime without knowing where the necessary financial resources would come from:

Mother simply went forward with the means at hand confident that God would supply what was lacking. "Don't worry," she would say with a smile, "if I were to think too much about procuring the means, the Lord would withhold his graces. We have nothing, yet we spend millions." No obstacle could stop her. She wrote, "Difficulties! What are they, Daughters? They are the mere playthings of children enlarged by our imagination, not yet accustomed to focus itself on the Omnipotent. Who is not weak? But with God's help you can do everything. He never fails the humble and faithful."[6]

Frances Xavier always said that when things got really difficult, God was about to do something especially wonderful. I try to imitate her faith on the road, but there is one hair-raising story about Cabrini that I have little hope of emulating. She was riding on a train in the Old West when her train was held up by robbers. One robber fired a pistol at her point-blank through the window, but the bullet dropped harmlessly to the floor beside her. St. Frances was unfazed and unsurprised. After all, hadn't she commended herself to the protection of the Sacred Heart?

Applying This Charism

The charism of Extraordinary Faith can be difficult to discern because people often get false positives when taking the inventory. Why? In our experience, most practicing Catholics know they are supposed to have "faith," but because the majority of

---

6 Dan Lynch, "A Missionary for our Time: Saint Frances Xavier Cabrini," *Catholic Exchange*, November 13, 2008 (online at http://catholicexchange.com/a-missionary-for-our-time-saint-frances-xavier-cabrini, as of May 5, 2017).

Catholics are not yet disciples, they do not know what a "normal" experience of living faith is like for a disciple. So, they can't distinguish between normal faith and a charism of Extraordinary Faith.

We have found that many lay Catholics who have ever made a costly decision or endured some inconvenience because of their faith tend to think of themselves as exceptional. Their Catholic family and friends often agree. Such behavior can certainly look extraordinary by comparison with the majority of Catholics who do not care and do not bother to show up. Because discipleship is not yet our living communal norm, they do not yet know that making hard choices is normal for disciples. For instance, prayer, fasting, and almsgiving at Lent are out of the ordinary when compared to the average American, but a Catholic who practices them is just being *normal*, not heroic.

People with the charism of Extraordinary Faith will often be found on the bleeding edge of mission. Extraordinary Faith is one of the two charisms most likely to be associated with starting a new group or apostolic initiative.

Evangelization and the Charism of Extraordinary Faith

When you are around somebody with Extraordinary Faith, your own faith in the presence, love, and power of God will grow. The evangelical power of Extraordinary Faith makes the Gospel come alive for other people in an intensely personal way.

People with this charism speak to those at every threshold. Their freedom to trust in extravagant ways builds trust, rouses curiosity, helps people dare to move into spiritual openness, and encourages seekers to really wrestle and finally have the courage to "drop their nets" and follow Jesus. Disciples living lives of extreme faith are often a great inspiration to emerging disciples and apostles as well.

Some Possible Expressions of Extraordinary Faith

- Fund-raiser
- Leader of cutting-edge organization or group
- Entrepreneur
- Founder
- Visionary
- Parent

THE CHARISM OF MISSIONARY

Definition

The charism of Missionary empowers a Christian to be a channel of God's goodness to others by effectively and joyfully using his or her charisms in a second culture.

Description

For most adults, learning another language and moving into a culture that is different from the one in which they were raised is very challenging and sometimes impossible. But people with the charism of Missionary are able to leap over this barrier and are energized by the challenge that involves far more than learning a new language. Becoming fully bi-cultural also requires the absorption of a host of customs — unwritten rules, tones of voice, gesture, dress, humor — that enable individuals to fruitfully use their other charisms in a new culture.

A Story of the Charism of Missionary

My friend Natali, an American who has lived in the Muslim world for over thirty years, once admitted to me with a guilty air: "I don't know if I'm wrong, but I feel closer to those Arab women than I do to many Westerners."

There is nothing wrong with her at all. Her unusual freedom to move cheerfully among these women, chatting easily in their language, as well as her ability to develop close friendships with numerous women and men of very different cultures, are all signs of a charism. She is routinely welcomed in places that no other Western woman goes, and Arabs who normally avoid foreigners delight in dropping in on her. She has been gifted by the Holy Spirit to move lightly across barriers that would prove insurmountable to many other disciples.

Applying This Charism

People with the charism of Missionary become quickly bored and frustrated in mono-cultural settings. They love the richness, color, and challenge of relating to and working with people from different cultures. The good news is that you don't have to go to another country to connect with people of another culture. Sometimes all you have to do these days is cross the street or begin a conversation at work, school, or with members of your own family. In the twenty-first century, this charism could also be exercised by disciples who can relate fruitfully to skeptics and unbelievers saturated in post-modern assumptions.

Evangelization and the Charism of Missionary

Disciples with a charism of Missionary care passionately about living, relating, and speaking in ways that make the Gospel intelligible and credible to the people from a different culture. People with a charism of Missionary are intensely sensitive to the nuances of the culture in which they seek to be a witness of Jesus Christ.

This charism is particularly useful in pre-evangelization, since this stage is all about building bridges of trust and rousing spiritual curiosity. It is also helpful when engaged in initial proclamation — telling Jesus' Great Story to those who have never heard it before — and in initiatory catechesis, because of its ability to leap over those cultural barriers.

Some Possible Expressions of Missionary

- Missionary
- International businessperson
- Diplomacy/reconciliation/peacemaker
- Worker with refugees or immigrants
- Worker with cultural or linguistic minority groups
- ESL (English as a Second Language) teacher

THE CHARISM OF VOLUNTARY POVERTY

Definition

Voluntary Poverty empowers a Christian to be a channel of God's loving presence by living a life of cheerful, voluntary simplicity or poverty in order to identify with Jesus and the poor.

Description

The charism of Voluntary Poverty is not *involuntary* poverty or simplicity of life. Poverty that is forced upon us by circumstances is no more voluntary poverty than getting robbed is the same as giving.

St. Paul tells us, "For you know the gracious act of our Lord Jesus Christ, that for your sake he became poor although he was rich, so that by his poverty you might become rich" (2 Corinthians 8:9). A person with the charism of Voluntary Poverty takes this understanding of the Incarnation seriously as a model for life.

Individuals with a charism of Voluntary Poverty feel uncomfortable when they have too much stuff. They are attracted to a life uncluttered by possessions and focused in simplicity on God and neighbor. Such freedom is, like all the Lifestyle charisms, a powerful witness to the liberty of the Gospel and frees one up to be used by God in out-of-the-box ways.

Stories of the Charism of Voluntary Poverty

Both St. Francis of Assisi (c. 1181-1226) and St. Dominic (1170-1221) lived lives of intentional, cheerful poverty and expected members of their respective orders to do the same. For St. Francis, the renunciation of worldly wealth and money was deeply personal. Francis' love of Lady Poverty was an end in itself. Christ was poor, and so Francis wanted to be poor.

Dominic's willingness to sacrifice for the sake of others began early; as a student, Dominic had sold his precious books to feed the poor. But for Dominic, a life of Voluntary Poverty was linked to mission. Dominic gladly embraced Voluntary Poverty in imitation of Christ, but he also did so for the sake of those scandalized by the clergy. Dominic knew that people were leaving the Church because of the laxness and worldliness of the Catholic clergy.

Francis' and Dominic's shared commitment to a lifestyle of poverty color all the stories about them. According to one famous story, Dominic was visiting Pope Innocent III in Rome. The Holy Father, pointing to the riches of the Church on display at St. Peter's, remarked, "Peter can no longer say, 'Silver and gold I do not have.'" To which Dominic replied, "Neither can he say, 'Rise and walk.'" There is another legend that St.

Dominic and St. Francis met in Rome and wished to exchange gifts with each other but had nothing to give since they were both so poor. So, they exchanged their belts. The cord belt of the Franciscan was originally the Dominican belt, and the leather belt of the Dominican was originally Franciscan.

Applying This Charism

This is a pretty rare charism at the parish level, so individuals with this gift can feel isolated and at odds with the values of other Catholics around them. When this gift (and a few others like Hospitality or Giving) emerges in the life of someone who is married, their spouse's first response can sometimes be "I didn't sign up for this." Husbands and wives will need to learn how to honor and support each other's charisms, even if they are surprising.

Evangelization and the Charism of Voluntary Poverty

Those with a charism of Voluntary Poverty can be very helpful at all the stages of the spiritual journey. Their witness is particularly effective in pre-evangelization and the early thresholds of trust, curiosity, and openness.

Some Possible Expressions of Voluntary Poverty

- Religious sister or brother
- Member of a third order or lay institute
- Missionary
- Exceptional giver
- Contemplative
- Influential prophetic figure

CHAPTER 8

Healing, Understanding, and Creative Charisms

"You are the light of the world. A city set on a mountain cannot be hidden. Nor do they light a lamp and then put it under a bushel basket; it is set on a lampstand, where it gives light to all in the house. Just so, your light must shine before others, that they may see your good deeds and glorify your heavenly Father."

MATTHEW 5:14-16

CHARISMS OF HEALING:

Focus is being a channel of God's healing and restoration.

- Healing
- Intercessory Prayer

THE CHARISM OF HEALING

Definition

The charism of Healing empowers a Christian to be a channel of God's love through whom God cures illness and restores health when healing is unlikely to occur quickly or to happen at all.

165

Description

What God does through a specific charism of Healing is different from the various kinds of healing made available through other charisms. All the charisms make the love of God present in some way — and where the love of God is present, healing occurs. But the charism of Healing (which is relatively rare) supernaturally empowers some people to heal others physically and emotionally in ways that clearly transcend normal clinical outcomes. Healing will occur much faster than normal or where healing is not expected to occur at all. The healing does not have to be medically inexplicable to be the fruit of this charism.

It is quite possible for a doctor, surgeon, nurse, or therapist to exercise a charism of Healing in addition to their acquired skill and experience. Their patient may receive standard treatment but experience a remarkable or even astonishing outcome.

A Story of the Charism of Healing

St. Martin de Porres (1579-1639) began life in Lima, Peru, as the unacknowledged son of a Spanish nobleman and a freed slave. He was apprenticed to a barber-physician as a boy. At that time, the law barred descendants of Africans and Indians from becoming full members of religious orders. The Dominican community accepted Martin at age fifteen as a *donado*, a volunteer who performed menial tasks in the monastery. Martin was finally allowed to take vows as a Dominican lay brother at twenty-four. Martin served the community as doctor, surgeon, and infirmarian, while he cared for the poor and sick of any class outside the priory.

Most of what we know about Martin's gift of healing comes from detailed eyewitness accounts given during his beatification process. Hundreds of astonishing cures as well as other miracles were attributed to him during his lifetime. For example, one of the priests in the community suffered from ulcers on his left leg. A local doctor treated him, but finally it was clear that the leg would have to be amputated. The operation was about to begin when Martin entered the room. He asked the surgeon to stop and said that he would heal the leg. In a few days, the friar was completely cured.[1]

My brother, Gary, is a gifted chiropractor who has pioneered new techniques and traveled around the world teaching them. He told me this story shortly after it happened. Ten years ago, he accompanied a team of volunteers from his church to build a house in an extremely poor Indian village in southern Baja.

Gary was treating local people when a frail woman was brought in who had suffered from a serious and very painful dislocation of the elbow for three years. Gary hesitated. There was no way to obtain an x-ray. Treating such a neglected injury in a woman who was already fragile without proper diagnostic tools is very tricky, and he was afraid that he would hurt her. As he struggled to decide what to do, a local pastor suggested that he pray. Gary did so, asking that the bones align themselves properly.

My brother said that the woman's arm started to quiver and then, with a loud pop that was heard throughout the room, the elbow slipped into place by itself. The woman had full strength and was pain-free almost immediately. The visiting team asked the woman to share her healing with the teenagers on the trip so that they would know that they could expect great things from God.

---

[1] *Butler's Lives of the Saints*, November, "St. Martin de Porres," revised by Sarah Fawcett Thomas (Collegeville, MN: The Liturgical Press, 1997), pp. 18-19.

Applying This Charism

One pattern that seems consistent with this charism is that the person exercising Healing needs some kind of contact with the person, preferably face-to-face, but sometimes over the phone or via Skype. That is one of the things that sets it apart from Intercessory Prayer.

Evangelization and the Charism of Healing

The evangelization focus of Healing is individuals. Few things communicate more clearly that a good and powerful God loves you than experiencing healing in one's own body or in that of a loved one or friend. A disciple with this charism can be especially helpful to skeptics and unbelievers as well as those at the thresholds of trust, curiosity, and openness.

Some Possible Expressions of Healing

- Priest
- Healing-prayer team member
- Eucharistic minister to the sick
- Medical professional
- Pastoral staff
- Helping professional

THE CHARISM OF INTERCESSORY PRAYER

Definition

The charism of Intercessory Prayer empowers the sustained, intense prayer of a Christian for others as the means by which God's love and deliverance reaches those in need.

Description

First of all, you do not need a charism of Intercessory Prayer to pray for someone else. Prayer for others is one of the spiritual works of mercy and does not require a special gift. Nonetheless, those who are given a charism of Intercessory Prayer tend to see remarkable — even miraculous — answers to their prayers for others on a regular basis. They have a tremendous confidence that God hears and will answer their prayers. They find praying for others energizing. Intercessory prayer is a crucial means by which God's love, provision, and deliverance reaches those in need.

A Story of the Charism of Intercessory Prayer

St. Thérèse of Lisieux (1873-1897) is one of the great models of Intercessory Prayer. Not only did she have this charism personally, but prayer for the needs of the Church is still an important part of the life of the Discalced Carmelite Order to which she belonged. Thérèse longed to be a missionary:

> But ... one mission alone would not be sufficient for me; I would want to preach the Gospel on all the five continents simultaneously and even to the most remote isles. I would be a missionary, not for a few years only, but from the beginning of creation until the consummation of the ages."[2]

Thérèse volunteered to be sent to establish a new Carmel in Vietnam but never left France because she became gravely

---

[2] *Patron and Patroness of the Missions* (online at http://phillymissions.org /mission-saints/patron-patroness-of-the-missions/, as of May 5, 2017).

ill. Thérèse died at age twenty-four without ever reaching the missions but has been named by the Church as patroness of all missionaries and the missions. She shares the honor with St. Francis Xavier as an intercessor who offered up her prayers, sufferings, and love for missionaries while on earth and still intercedes for them in heaven.[3]

Applying This Charism

We are called, as the Church, to intercede intensely for the renewal of our parish and diocese and for the establishment of God's kingdom in our world.

Pope Francis writes:

> The great men and women of God were great intercessors. Intercession is like a "leaven" in the heart of the Trinity. It is a way of penetrating the Father's heart and discovering new dimensions which can shed light on concrete situations and change them. We can say that God's heart is touched by our intercession, yet in reality he is always there first. What our intercession achieves is that his power, his love and his faithfulness are shown ever more clearly in the midst of the people.[4]

Evangelization and the Charism of Intercessory Prayer

The charism of Intercessory Prayer[5] is important at all the thresholds but especially when someone is on the verge of spiritual openness and intentional discipleship. That's because all sorts of interior and exterior obstacles begin to emerge in the

---

[3] Ibid.
[4] Pope Francis, *Evangelii Gaudium*, 283.
[5] For more on the charism of Intercessory Prayer, see chapter 9.

lives and hearts of people who are passing through these crisis points of decision.[6]

In addition to this kind of intercession for *individuals*, the need for organized *corporate* intercession is essential to pre-evangelization of the larger community and for the spiritual renewal of the parish. Such prayer is crucial to this work because it *changes the spiritual atmosphere of a place or community*. Intercessory prayer also fosters the spiritual openness of individuals, even those who just happen to "drop by" our parish, home, or office cubicle.

Some Possible Expressions of Intercessory Prayer

- Rosary/Novena
- Prayer chain
- Eucharistic Adoration
- RCIA team member
- Healing-prayer team
- Parent/grandparent

CHARISMS OF UNDERSTANDING:
Focus is understanding the ways of God and humanity.

- Knowledge
- Wisdom

THE CHARISM OF KNOWLEDGE

Definition

Knowledge empowers a Christian to be a channel of God's truth through diligent, prayerful study and intellectual inquiry

---

[6]   Weddell, *Forming Intentional Disciples*, pp. 159, 180.

that enables us to better understand God, ourselves, and the universe.

Description

The charism of Knowledge is supernaturally empowered study. It is not just reading books or acquiring information. And though great intellectuals like St. Albert the Great and St. Thomas Aquinas manifested this charism, you don't have to be a professional academic to exercise this gift. The foundational passion for those with a charism of Knowledge is intellectual wonder, and you can follow it freely into realms as diverse as philosophy, theology, metaphysics, mathematics, or any of the other natural sciences.

Those with a charism of Knowledge want to uncover and contemplate the great truths behind the universe. They understand that those truths do not have to have an immediate practical application to be of enormous value. As one Dominican friend told me with considerable fire in the middle of a theological discussion, "*It's practical because it's true!*"

For those with the charism of Knowledge, study is a major form of prayer. Dr. John Medina, a molecular biologist, summed it up beautifully when he described his laboratory bench as his "second altar."[7] Knowledge is a charism particularly common among and honored by Dominicans.

A Story of the Charism of Knowledge

Eighteen-year-old Jacques Maritain (1882-1973) met seven-teen-year-old Raïssa Oumansov (1883-1960) at the Univer-

---

[7] "John Medina: Putting Your Face Against the Face of God," *Wittenburg Door*, #119 (September/October 1991).

sity of Paris in the fall of 1900 and fell in love. Jacques was an agnostic from a non-practicing French Protestant background and Raïssa was an agnostic from a Russian Jewish family, and both were on an intellectual and spiritual quest. They made a pact that if they had not found "the immutable truth that would demand their entire allegiance"[8] within a reasonable amount of time, they would commit suicide together.

Happily, within a year they had encountered the philosophy of Henri Bergson, which prepared them to encounter the Catholic faith into which they were baptized in 1906. Subsequently, they became the godparents to a wide circle of converts in France. Jacques and Raïssa ran Thomist study groups in their home for twenty years for both Catholic and Catholic-friendly seekers desiring to wrestle with and integrate the intellect and faith. Many of France's cutting-edge artists, musicians, intellectuals, and theologians participated, and a number were baptized in the Maritains' private chapel.

Jacques had a huge influence throughout the Catholic world, through his books and lectures. Raïssa, who was physically frail, was also a writer, poet, and contemplative. Jacques called Raïssa "half my soul." The Maritains both seem to have been given a charism of Knowledge, so the search for ultimate truth was at the center of their Catholic faith and their life together.

Applying This Charism

Knowledge, like all the charisms, is for the benefit of others. The question is, "How will you share this charism with others?" What other charisms have you been given that may provide a way for you to share the truth you see? People with the gift

---

[8] Judith D. Suther, *Raïssa Maritain: Pilgrim, Poet, Exile* (New York: Fordham University Press, 1990), p. 20.

of Knowledge often end up in academic settings or perhaps involved with intellectually and culturally sophisticated apologetics. Apostles with this charism contribute brilliantly to the pre-evangelization of the culture as well.

Evangelization and the Charism of Knowledge

Someone with the charism of Knowledge can be enormously helpful working with intellectually oriented skeptics, agnostics, atheists, academics, and those for whom *truth* is the transcendental that will most readily lead them to encountering God. They can also help form disciples and apostles for mission in a skeptical world and in academic settings.

Some Possible Expressions of Knowledge

- Teacher
- Preacher
- Scholar/scientist
- Leader (especially of educational or high-tech organization)
- Writer
- Home-schooling parent

THE CHARISM OF WISDOM

Definition

Wisdom empowers a Christian to be a channel of God's goodness through extraordinary insight that enables him or her to come up with original or creative solutions to specific problems and to make good decisions.

Description

The charisms of Knowledge and Wisdom are sometimes confused with each other. Wisdom focuses on inspired, creative solutions to practical problems. Wisdom is all about the *creative application of knowledge* in order to better the lives of human beings and build the Kingdom of God. It is *not* enough for a Wisdom person that something simply be objectively true. It must also be applicable in a way that makes a significant difference in the lives of real people and brings glory to God.

Wisdom is the gift of extraordinary problem-solving insight that is triggered by an encounter with and understanding of a real-life problem that cries out for a solution. One of the signs of this charism is that a deep understanding of negative realities doesn't depress you but sparks your energy and creativity, because you know that contemplating a problem is the first step toward finding an elegant, transforming solution. You do not need an academic background to exercise this charism.

A Story of the Charism of Wisdom

A wonderful example of the charism of Wisdom is Caroline Chisholm (1808-1877), a Catholic whose creative problem-solving is legendary in Australia. Caroline was raised as an English Protestant but married a Catholic army officer and was received into the Church as a young woman. Caroline's husband, Archie, was posted to Australia in 1838 and Caroline went with him.

Australia had been founded as a penal colony, where convicted British criminals were transported to work off their sentence instead of being sent to prison or the gallows. In 1840, the ratio of men to women in Australia was still almost three to one. To attract more women immigrants, subsidized passage to Australia was offered to any British or Irish woman who wanted to begin a new life "down under."

Thousands took up the offer, but no one had made sufficient provision for the women when they arrived. Penniless, single immigrant girls unable to find a job within ten days of arrival were forced to leave the ship and found themselves on their own. Many women were met at the dock by local madams or men and were quickly trapped in some form of sexual or other slavery. Caroline witnessed this and knew that something needed to be done.

Caroline asked the governor for use of an empty warehouse in Sydney. The public hue and cry about a young immigrant girl who had just been found unconscious and starving on the street made the reluctant governor see reason, and he gave Caroline the key. She spent the first night in the warehouse sitting on her bed, watching rats eating her bread ration. The next day, she poisoned the rats and began the task of overhauling the building and turning it into a giant dormitory.

Caroline had already sent out notices all over the region, inquiring about potential jobs for female workers. Within days, ninety immigrant women filled the warehouse. Caroline interviewed the women about their history, skills, and work experience. She set their employment contracts and work conditions. On her white horse, Caroline led caravans of young women far out into the bush, dropping them off at their new homes on farms, cattle stations, and in hamlets. Caroline ultimately found jobs for 11,000 women and became known throughout Australia as the "Immigrant's Friend."

Her husband, Archie, was very supportive. Caroline and Archie once came across a group of newly arrived, penniless Scottish Highlanders who spoke no English. Archie, who was very generous, immediately pulled out his wallet. Caroline's gift was a practical suggestion: What if they used some of the money to buy axes and rope? Then they could rent a cart and cut and sell wood to the local inns and become independent. A few days later, Archie and Caroline saw the Highlanders delivering wood on a handcart.

Applying This Charism

People with this charism often find themselves sought out by those who want to talk over the issues and situations they are facing. People with this charism are often brilliant at diagnosis and prescription. Where the rest of us see chaos, they see *patterns*, and therefore possible *causes* — and therefore possible *remedies*. Disciples exercising a charism of Wisdom are usually able to sum up the situation in clear, illuminating language. The words "insight" and "clarity" are often used to describe them. The insights that flow from the charism can have an almost prophetic force (even when delivered quietly) but simultaneously restore hope and provide direction for the future.

Evangelization and the Charism of Wisdom

The gift of Wisdom can be enormously helpful when it comes to evangelizing cultures. Wisdom people can have a major cultural impact because they can have tremendous insight into the broader cultural, economic, political, and social issues of their day. They can be especially helpful in understanding where non-believers are coming from, with their very different questions, doubts, and fears.

Some Possible Expressions of Wisdom

- Leader
- Teacher/preacher

- Writer
- Counselor
- Diplomat
- Innovator or inventor

THE CREATIVE CHARISMS:

Focus is creative activity that orders and beautifies.

- Craftsmanship
- Music
- Writing

THE CHARISM OF CRAFTSMANSHIP

Definition

Craftsmanship empowers a Christian to be an effective channel of God's goodness to others through sacred or secular artistic creativity that beautifies and orders the physical world.

Description

I have defined the charism of Craftsmanship broadly because it serves as the spark of an enormous variety of faith-shaped arts ranging from painting the Sistine Chapel to filmmaking, and from embroidery to cooking to architecture. Craftsmanship glorifies God by creating beauty that nourishes all that is fully human, whether it is expressed in a sacred or a secular setting. The art created with this gift need not be explicitly religious for it to impact others for God's purposes. We can use such a charism in a setting where nobody around us believes what we believe, and we can do so to the glory of God.

When the great Russian novelist Fyodor Dostoyevsky observed that "Beauty will save the world," he did not mean that all artists and aesthetes are saints. Instead, he meant that power of this gift touches the whole of us and baptizes our imaginations and our senses. When people encounter the beauty that comes through this charism, they are encountering the Beauty who is Christ, whether they know it or not.

A Story of the Charism of Craftsmanship

Ade Bethune (1914-2002) was a devout nineteen-year-old, emerging Catholic artist when she first met Dorothy Day in New York City. Ade created many famous woodcuts of worker saints and the corporal works of mercy for the *Catholic Worker* newspaper. She welcomed poor young women as apprentices into her home and trained them in both the fine arts and the arts of living. Ade brought the same creative intensity to cooking and gardening as to sculpture, painting, crafting mosaics, carving wood, and liturgical art. Dorothy Day said of Ade, "Whenever I visited Ade, I came away with a renewed zest for life. She has such a sense of the sacramentality of life, the goodness of things...."[9]

Applying This Charism

Craftsmanship is not simply being handy. The heart and soul of this gift is creating beauty. For those who are given this gift, creating beauty is a major form of prayer and a critical part of their spiritual life.

Evangelization and the Charism of Craftsmanship

The power of the charism of Craftsmanship speaks to the hearts of individuals, but it can also be exercised as a form of pre-

---

[9] Dorothy Day, *The Long Loneliness* (New York: Orbis Books, 1952), p. 217.

evangelization that shapes a whole culture in a way that fosters human flourishing and sets the stage for people to encounter God. Craftsmanship helps build bridges of trust, evokes spiritual curiosity, and helps people move into openness.

Some Possible Expressions of Craftsmanship

- Painter/sculptor
- Creative homemaker
- Cook/chef
- Interior designer/architect
- Landscape designer/gardener
- Iconographer

THE CHARISM OF MUSIC

Definition

The charism of Music empowers a Christian to be a channel of God's creative goodness to others through writing or performing music for the delight of others and the praise of God.

Description

The music that is produced by a disciple exercising this charism does not have to be religious or overtly spiritual music. It can be jazz, rock, classical, or country. The music can be of any genre, played in a secular or religious setting, and still impact people and open them up to the presence of God.

Stories of the Charism of Music

Giovanni Pierluigi da Palestrina (c. 1525-1594) lived in Rome with his wife. There he met and became a disciple of St. Philip Neri, the beloved apostle of the city. Neri understood the great power of music to move people spiritually. He incorporated it into many events, from his community's informal weekly gatherings to his creative Mardi Gras alternative: a pilgrimage to visit the seven major churches of Rome combined with a musical picnic.

Palestrina served as director of Neri's choir and wrote many *laude* — vernacular praise songs — for the Oratory's weekly gatherings. As a composer of music for the Mass, Palestrina had no peer. He became the greatest musical voice of the Catholic Reformation, and his music is still cherished and performed at St. Peter's Basilica and all over the world.

I once interviewed a gifted man who received high scores in both Craftsmanship and Music. He was very clear about which of those scores reflected a genuine charism. I asked, "How do you know?" He responded, "I built my own log house and it is beautiful. Lots of people compliment me on it, but it has nothing to do with my relationship with God. On the other hand, singing is pure prayer for me. And when I sing, other people are moved to prayer as well."

Applying This Charism

If this is your charism, Music will be a major form of prayer and spiritual discipline for you. You do *not* have to be a professional or have had extensive training to exercise this charism.

Evangelization and the Charism of Music

Because it speaks to human hearts at all stages of life and in every culture, the charism of Music can be powerful in pre-evangelization, during initial proclamation where it can be a form of proclaiming the Gospel, and as part of initiatory catechesis. It can also nourish and strengthen the faith of maturing disciples and apostles.

Some Possible Expressions of Music

- Professional musician
- Music therapist/educator
- Worship leader
- Music ministry in a parish or small Christian community
- Composer or arranger
- Director of musical groups

THE CHARISM OF WRITING

Definition

Writing empowers a Christian to be a channel of God's creativity by using words to create works of truth or beauty that reflect the fullness of human experience and bring glory to God.

Description

Writing is a tricky charism to discern, because if you are reading this book, you are literate and many of us have spent years writing at school and work. We have to distinguish between all that training, skill, and experience and the presence of a genuine charism. If writing is a charism, it will often feel like prayer or contemplation at the moment you are engaged in it and will be a major spiritual discipline for you.

A Story of the Charism of Writing

Flannery O'Connor (1925-1964) is known for her stories filled with grotesque characters and biting satire, set in the American South. Raised Catholic in a small town in Georgia, as a young woman O'Connor moved to New York to write. She was diagnosed with lupus a few years later and returned home, where she continued to write. Flannery's Catholic faith was central to her life and informed her stories at a deep level, even though they were not overtly Catholic. She once remarked that if the South was not deeply Christian, it was certainly Christ-haunted — and so were her stories.

Applying This Charism

We need to discern between the exceptional impact of a charism of Writing and simply exercising the skill of writing for other purposes. Using words to create beauty or convey truth is at the heart of the charism of Writing. On the other hand, the skill of a literate person can be used as a platform to express many different charisms: Knowledge, Wisdom, Teaching, Encouragement, and so on. The impact of one's writing will vary according to the charism at work.

For instance, I worked with one woman who thought she might have a charism of Writing, but when I listened to her stories, I realized that something else was going on. She loved to write encouraging cards to total strangers whose troubles she read about in her local newspaper. It quickly become clear that she was probably exercising the *charism of Encouragement* via the *skill of writing*. She was not focused upon creating beauty with words; she was seeking, with her words, to encourage and strengthen people who were experiencing tragedy.

Evangelization and the Charism of Writing

C. S. Lewis once remarked that reading the stories of George MacDonald baptized his imagination long before his heart and mind were ready to follow. St. Augustine described the turning point of his conversion this way: "I heard from a neighboring house a voice, as of boy or girl, I know not, chanting, and oft repeating, 'Take up and read; Take up and read.'"[10]

God can use the Charism of Writing, in powerful ways, in people at any of the thresholds of pre-discipleship, as well as to change the lives of those who have already begun the journey of missionary discipleship.

Some Possible Expressions of Writing

- Novelist/poet
- Dramatist/screenwriter
- Journalist
- Public relations professional
- Editor/ghostwriter
- Speechwriter

---

[10] St. Augustine of Hippo, *Confessions*, chapter 12 (online at https://www.ccel.org/ccel/augustine/confess.ix.xii.html, as of May 5, 2017).

CHAPTER 9

The Art of Discerning Charisms

While trying the spirits to see if they be of God, priests should uncover with a sense of faith, acknowledge with joy and foster with diligence the various humble and exalted charisms of the laity.

PRESBYTERORUM ORDINIS, 9

In 2012, I wrote:

> The spiritual forces unleashed in the Christian community through conversion and ongoing discipleship will evoke and, in a real sense, demand governance.[1]

The charisms are an essential part of those spiritual forces. No wonder the Church teaches that a critical part of the pastoral office is to recognize, uncover with faith, acknowledge with joy, foster with diligence, appreciate, judge and discern, coordinate and put to good use, and have "heartfelt esteem" for all the charisms of all the baptized.[2]

---

[1] Weddell, *Forming Intentional Disciples*, p. 85.

[2] *Presbyterorum Ordinis* (Decree on the Ministry and Life of Priests), 9 (online at http://www.vatican.va/archive/hist_councils/ii_vatican_council /documents/vat-ii_decree_19651207_presbyterorum-ordinis_en.html, as of May 5, 2017); *Lumen Gentium*, 30; Pope St. John Paul II, *Pastores Dabo Vobis* 40, 74; Pope St. John Paul II, *Christifideles Laici*, 32.

First, to "uncover a charism with faith" means that since this person has been baptized, we can take the word of the Church that the graces which attend baptism have been poured out — including the grace of charisms. Our task is to help what God has certainly placed in the person to manifest, emerge, and be recognized.

Second, to acknowledge a genuine charism with joy is to celebrate and thank God for bringing his gifts to birth in the person. We rejoice in the blessing these gifts will be to the Church and the world when the person manifests these charisms — even if it is a gift that you or I don't have and don't intuitively understand. (We'll get to the issue of how to recognize a genuine charism in a moment.)

Finally, to foster a charism with diligence means that we cannot be passive. We are to be proactive in cooperating with grace by putting time, money, energy, and resources into fostering the discernment of all the baptized, not merely sitting back and waiting for gifted apostles to spontaneously emerge.

Disciples and apostles do not "just happen." In the garden of the Church, vocations do not "just happen." *Weeds happen.* Disciples, apostles, and vocations are the result of *sustained prayer, planning, and evangelization by a Christian community.* A critical part of the whole is intentionally helping disciples uncover their gifts with a sense of faith, acknowledge genuine charisms with joy, and foster their discernment and exercise with diligence.

Discernment of charisms is supposed to happen within the Christian community. Roughly 98 percent of Catholics around the world have no access to a lay movement or a religious community. Nothing, practically speaking, comes close to the potential impact of the parish — far and away the most common institution in the Catholic world — in forming and supporting the laity for their part in our common mission. The parish plays an essential role in preparing apostles with a variety of charisms and vocations to bring Christ to the whole world.

A Basic Introduction

I created and gave the first Called & Gifted workshop as a volunteer. I knew almost nothing, but I wasn't able to find any existing Catholic resources — so I did my best and learned from my many mistakes. My collaborators and I have been listening, learning, and constantly updating the Called & Gifted discernment process ever since. This is a very basic introduction to what we have learned about how to fruitfully facilitate the discernment of individual charisms in a parish setting.

The discernment process has three essential steps.

First, we offer a live introductory workshop that introduces the Church's theology of charisms and the basics of discernment.[3] In the near future, we will be creating an updated version of the introductory workshop that can be streamed via our website. In the context of the workshop, participants take the *Catholic Spiritual Gifts Inventory* to help them identity the most promising places to begin discernment.

The introductory workshop prepares you to dive into the second phase: a personal, one-on-one interview with someone who is trained to listen to your experiences and hear the signs of your charisms in your stories. Interviewers review your inventory results, help you discern the patterns in your life that point to the possible presence of one or more charisms, and help you choose a charism to actively discern.

---

[3] To find out where live Called & Gifted workshops are being offered around the United States and elsewhere, visit our event calendar page at http://www.siena.org.

Finally, the third step is actual experimentation and small-group discernment. We strongly recommend that each discerner choose a possible charism to experiment with for a minimum of two hours a week over at least six to eight weeks. Ideally, those discerning get together with other discerners and facilitators every other week and talk about their experiences and what they are learning. It is in the course of this third step that the light really begins to dawn for many people.

But first, I must explain the number one, essential rule of the discernment road: *Taking an inventory is not discernment!*

I once received a call from a parish leader who ordered 500 copies of the *Catholic Spiritual Gifts Inventory*. She explained that her plan was to sit outside the sanctuary during Mass, flag down parishioners as they left, sit them down, and have them take the inventory on the spot — and then she would know "where to put them." I listened in disbelief, thinking, "Where do I begin?"

It was the beginning of a steep learning curve about the American fixation with testing. I was doing a Called & Gifted workshop in North Carolina's Research Triangle a few years ago. The room was filled with high-powered scientists, researchers, and physicians who approached taking the inventory as though they were taking the MCAT or GRE again. The tension in the room was unbearable. I was sure that some of them were working their inventory results out to the ninth decimal place. I knew they were going to be very unhappy when I told them the same thing I have learned to say to every person who has just taken the inventory:

"Now I have to tell you that your inventory scores are bogus."

As always, I waited in silence for several seconds for the penny to drop. When it did, the disbelief on the faces of this crowd of type-A uber-achievers was indescribable.

What do I mean by "bogus"? I mean *taking the inventory is not discernment.* Why?

Because charisms are *real*; they are not fantasies or projections of our unresolved issues on the universe. The charisms are graces of God that enter the world through our assent and cooperation, and they change history in ways that other people can recognize. The only way to discern an individual charism[4] is to take action and see what God does through your obedience.

The sole purpose of the inventory is to help people get into the discernment process fast. An inventory is just a tool that enables a large number of people with very different spiritual and life experiences to each identify the most likely place to *begin* their personal discernment in a short amount of time. The inventory is a quick-and-dirty way to sort through your life experience to this point and identify the most fruitful places to start discernment. That is all. Which is why I joke while explaining what the inventory scores mean,

> "*Please* do not go to your pastor on Sunday and announce, 'I got a "15" in Pastoring. Step aside, Father!' They'll never let us back in the diocese again."

In our instant Google culture, I have had to disappoint a lot of people who just want to cut to the chase, take the inventory, and "get their scores." Our faith in such instruments is touching — and so American. People who don't understand the realities sometimes put inventories online for people to take without any context or assistance. (Indeed, I've had people try to pass my inventory off as their own and put it online!) Others urged

---

[4] The discernment of an individual charism is different from that of a founding charism or a hierarchical charism. See chapter 4 for more on the distinctions between the different types of charisms.

me to cut the inventory's 120 questions to 30 and create a phone app. Behold: insta-discernment on your phone while waiting for the barista to make your grande caramel macchiato. No! A thousand times, no! There is an app for nearly everything, but *not* for discerning charisms!

What we call "raw," undiscerned inventory scores are affected by all kinds of things: where you are in your relationship with God, the depth and breadth of your life experience, your personality, how self-critical you are, how you were feeling at the moment you took the inventory, how you interpreted the wording of the question, etc. We always remind people that ending up with a higher score than your friend does *not* mean that you are more gifted, so please don't compare scores.

When I ask a person I'm interviewing what they were thinking about when they answered a particular question a certain way, their first answer is sometimes, "I don't know." More than one person has told me ruefully, "I have *no* idea why I gave that answer. I must have had a TIA (a mini-stroke)!" Usually, one or more "high" scores will be eliminated as irrelevant by the end of your personal interview, while one or more second-tier scores often turn out to point to a possible charism. If you try to take your inventory results in isolation as final, you will almost certainly end up with a distorted picture of your possible charisms.

Which brings us to the second essential rule of the discernment road:

> *The fastest way to guarantee that exploring your charisms does not bear fruit is to insist on instant answers without any sustained real-life discernment.* (This is why I have not included the *Catholic Spiritual Gifts Inventory* in this book.)

So how does one discern a charism?

THE FIVE STEPS OF DISCERNMENT

1. Explore the Possibilities

Most Catholics do not yet know that they have been given charisms. We have learned to presume that it is a brand-new idea for the majority. Our goal in our initial workshop is to give people the background and basic knowledge that they need to begin a discernment process immediately.

2. Experiment

Choose one possible charism and experiment with it for a minimum of two hours a week over at least six to eight weeks. We have found all three parts of the discernment process build upon one another and that most substantive clarification happens during the extended discernment process.

The classic Nike motto sums it up well: "Just do it!" You have to *do* it and see what God does! I've watched numerous people go through whole ten-week extended discernment processes but never take action. They were no clearer about their charisms at the end than when they began.

Part of experimenting is exercising your charism for someone else. If you wonder whether you have a charism of Mercy, you need to spend time helping those who suffer in a direct, hands-on fashion. If you want to discern a charism of Music, you have to make music where someone else can hear you. Singing in the shower doesn't count. If you think you may have a charism of Writing, the only way to find out is to put your writing out there where other people can read it. Writing in code that only the FBI can break and storing it in an encrypted file is not going to get you where you want to go.

There are a few exceptions to that general rule. As I mentioned in chapter 8, lifestyle charisms like Celibacy, Extraordinary Faith, Missionary, and Voluntary Poverty can't be discerned in two hours a week. Definitive discernment can take up to a year or even longer depending upon the nature of the charism you are exploring and the opportunities available to you.

And as you experiment, you need to keep your eyes open for the three classic signs of a charism, one of which is *subjective*, and two of which are *objective*.

The Experience of Exercising a Charism
The first sign is:

3. Your Experience
What is it like to exercise a charism? First of all, we are typically energized when using our charisms. The charisms are the Holy Spirit's great remedy for burnout. We have never met anyone who has burned out in the exercise of their charisms. To be sure, you can burn out from activities *around* the exercise of your charism. I know people who are truly gifted in Teaching, but the institutional politics wear them out or they struggle with the parent-teacher conferences. But that is not the test of a charism of Teaching.

The test of a charism is what happens at the moment you are doing the activity in question, *not* getting ready to do it and *not* cleaning up afterward. At the moment that someone with the charism is engaged in teaching, they are usually full of energy. The renewed energy that accompanies the exercise of one's charisms is part of what makes it possible for disciples to stay the course over the long haul.

Second, when we exercise our charisms we feel like we have "found our place" or that we "fit." There is a sense that we are where we belong even if we are doing something for the very first time or are in a situation that is wholly new to us.

Third, it is very common for people to experience a sense of joyful satisfaction while they are exercising their charisms. I had an amusing experience of working with a man who was discerning what he thought might be a charism of Administration. He was taking the Called & Gifted workshop in an effort to figure what he could do after he retired. As I was listening to him, I noticed that when he talked about actually organizing a group to undertake a complicated task, his face and body language changed dramatically. He was not joyful and energized but depressed and slouching. So, I asked him if he would voluntarily do further administrative work when he retired. His response was immediate: "Never! Never again!" Why had he scored high in the charism of Administration on the inventory? Because administration was part of his responsibilities at work. He did it because he had to, not because he was graced to do it.

Fourth, we often have a sense of the presence of God when using a charism. Exercising charisms can often feel like prayer or contemplation. When I help people discern their charisms, I often ask, "How is this charism related to your lived relationship with God?" Some people just beam and pour out the story of God's love and presence that they experience when using their gift. At other times, I get the deer-in-the-headlights look, and it quickly becomes clear that this particular person does not know what to say.

It is a significant red flag when there is no apparent connection between a possible charism and a person's relationship with God. Perhaps the activity in question is not a charism at all but simply a human skill. Maybe the individual is just doing this activity because his or her job or family requires it. Or perhaps, it is simply that this person does not yet have what he or she would recognize as a relationship with God. Whatever the obstacle, it is very possible that you are *not* dealing with a charism.

It is vital to remember that a person can have a very negative experience the first time he or she experiments with a particular charism, and that is *not* discernment. Remember, we are looking for patterns *over time*: months or even years. You cannot discern a charism in an hour or a day.

For instance, I fainted out of sheer terror the first time I spoke in public. Obviously, if that was a recurring pattern in my life, I wouldn't be doing this work since my co-teachers would get really tired of picking me up off the floor every time I tried to teach. It is true for many of us that our greatest fears are sometimes wrapped around our greatest gifts. When we approach that charism, our fear can rise up and nearly overwhelm us. But that is not discernment. Some of us will have to push past our initial anxieties to discover if there is a charism behind those fears.

There is no charism that is given to the majority of the baptized. It is always a minority experience. Anyone who is given a charism may feel a bit or even very different from the majority of the baptized. Some gifts are only given to a tiny minority (say 1 percent), while other charisms will be much more common (perhaps 20 percent). So far as I know, there are no studies or precise numbers about how the charisms are distributed. But we know there is no charism shared by the majority. So, as Paul says:

> If they were all one part, where would the body be? But as it is, there are many parts, yet one body. The eye cannot say to the hand, "I do not need you," nor again the head to the feet, "I do not need you." (1 Corinthians 12:19-21)

When the Church says, "You have a unique contribution to make to the Church's mission," she is quite serious.

To sum up the first sign of a charism, exercising a charism is typically energizing, satisfying, and joyful. At the moment, you are using a charism, you feel like you are where you belong, that it is an expression of your relationship with God. Exercising a charism often feels like prayer or contemplation. These feelings will not necessarily be present every single time, but they will definitely be characteristic of the experience of exercising a genuine charism *over time*.

Personal experience is often the first sign that we become aware of, but it is not the only sign or even the most important.

4. Evaluate Your Effectiveness

The single most important sign of a charism is simple: What does God do through your gift? A charism does what it is supposed to do. If you have a charism of Healing, people get well. If they are worse off after you are done, it's a clue! If you have a charism of Leadership, people will buy into your vision of a better future and work together to make the vision happen.

When you explore a possible charism but see only mediocre or poor fruits, that is not failure. That is really useful data. It is a success, not a failure, to know where we are not gifted! It suggests that your charisms lie elsewhere. Success in discernment is recognizing where you *are* gifted and where you are *not*. Both "ahas" are a normal part of the discernment process. Eliminating charism possibilities frees us up to focus on those areas where we are genuinely called and gifted.

Some of those who attend our workshops are members of the "Core" — the 4 percent of adult Catholics who make everything happen. Some have been on parish staff for years. Others have served as ushers, catechists, members of the pastoral council, and pillars of the St. Vincent de Paul Society. They've set up the tables, made the coffee, and worked the fish fries. They have done *everything*. But they do not have charisms in all those areas and need to discern where their ministry is bearing exceptional fruit. On the other hand, some who show up for our workshops are the quiet ones who sit in the back of the church, and parish leaders don't even know who they are. All will have to distinguish between their life experience, their natural talents and skills, and the presence of one or more supernaturally fruitful charisms. This leads to the final step.

5. Expect (and Look for) Feedback from Others

Feedback can be both *direct* and *indirect*. *Direct feedback* happens when people have the language to talk about charisms. If a friend of yours was familiar with charisms, they might come to you and say, "Do you remember how you helped me when I felt so depressed last winter? You listened to me and talked with me, and I felt so much better afterward. I was wondering if maybe you have a charism of Encouragement?"

There are different kinds of direct feedback. Father Michael was once surrounded by a group of parishioners who wanted to know if he could help them figure out how to convince their friend Tom that he did *not* have a charism of Music, because listening to him was killing them! Tom was obviously having a good time, but he was not taking in all his clues.

Indirect feedback is more subtle. It is one of the mysteries of grace that others can often recognize your gifts even if you don't know what they are. A schoolteacher told me that her students came up and asked her to pray for their healing. She asked, "How do they know? I've never told them that I have a gift of healing." This is an example of *indirect feedback*. We don't know how this works but have long observed that other people can sense our charisms. Somehow, they intuit them or perhaps are inspired by the Holy Spirit to just come and ask for the grace we have been given to give. Indirect feedback is when people vote with their feet and come up and ask you for your gift.

One of the common challenges of helping people take in the feedback of others is that many cradle Catholics, especially women, tend to filter out positive feedback. As one woman from the Upper Midwest told me, "Oh, I know what my charism is; but I got so much positive feedback about that, I stopped using it in case I got proud." The only possible reply to this sort of misplaced humility is, "Sweetheart, it's not about you."

This kind of "humility" definitely gets in the way of discernment. There is no reason to be more self-conscious about acknowledging that God has given you a charism than you would feel about letting someone know that you are baptized. If all the baptized receive charisms (whether manifested or not), why do you imagine that a matter-of-fact acknowledgement of their presence makes you special or sets you apart in any way at all? You might as well be afraid of showing off if you mention that you have a driver's license. If you are sixteen, we understand your excitement. But if you are still flashing your driver's license at twenty-five, you need to get a life.

When, in the name of humility, we neglect or refuse to give away our gifts to others, we are not pleasing God. We are the stewards of these graces; we hold them for others. Recognizing and exercising them for others is a form of obedience.

Another common discernment issue is brought up by the declaration, "I have no charisms," which was uttered by one woman in a particularly memorable interview. Since we have learned from long experience not to argue about things like that, I just moved ahead. Looking at her inventory, I noted that she had a few high scores in Hospitality, so I asked her why she had answered the way she did.

For a moment, she was truly flummoxed. She couldn't think of a single thing. After a few minutes of silence, she said, "Well … thirteen years ago, there was a refugee family who needed a place to stay and they came and stayed with us." I perked up. This was promising. It was only when she confessed that the same refugee family *was still living with her thirteen years later* that I begin to grasp the depth of her denial. She turned out to have a massive charism of Hospitality, which I am sure that everyone in her life could have confirmed.

The ease and grace with which she welcomed people into her home and life all seemed so normal to her that she didn't even have a name for it. This is another reason why we need feedback from other people. A charism can seem quite ordinary to the one exercising it. Other people who do not have that charism can remind us that, in fact, not everyone can do the things we do.

If you have a charism of Hospitality, the indirect feedback you will typically receive is that your family, friends, parishioners all want to hang out at your place, and they comment upon what a difference spending time there makes. One friend with a charism of Wisdom just keeps an empty chair beside her desk because throughout the day, co-workers drop in to run their problems by her and get her insights. Her co-workers are telling her what they were receiving from her without words. To discern, you have to give yourself permission to see the evidence that God is using your obedience for good.

TIME TO COME TO A CONCLUSION

The three signs of a charism — your personal experience, your objective effectiveness for the Kingdom of God, and the positive feedback of others, both direct and indirect, should be consistently present over time. This is why you need months to discern a charism and why you cannot do so by just taking an inventory. If all three signs are present on a consistent basis, it is very likely that you are dealing with a charism.

However, if only one or two of the signs are present regularly, if you are receiving "mixed signals" even though you have been discerning seriously over a matter of months, there comes the point when it is time to come to a conclusion, as in "I don't think I have a charism of Helps."

One reason that it is a success to understand where you are not gifted is that eliminating one possibility often makes other genuine possibilities more visible. I have heard many discerners say something like, "I can't believe that I didn't see the pattern before. I'm not working out of a charism of Helps. It's a charism of Service."

CHARISMS TYPICALLY WELCOMED AND FOSTERED IN PAROCHIAL SETTINGS

One of our unexpected discoveries is that, in the average parish, our current cultural norms tend to encourage and foster the growth of some charisms while suppressing and discouraging others. Charisms typically encouraged in an average parish include:

- Administration
- Craftsmanship
- Mercy
- Encouragement
- Music
- Giving
- Pastoring
- Helps
- Service
- Hospitality
- Wisdom

The reason these charisms are affirmed and welcomed is not hard to understand. They are charisms useful for the liturgy, for nurturing and caring for people, and for maintaining structures. Since most parishes are ordered toward inward maintenance rather than outward mission, there is a sort of unconscious natural selection process occurring. Pastors and other leaders naturally appreciate and encourage those people with charisms that facilitate two very important functions: keeping the ecclesial trains running on time and the pastoral care of individuals and families.

CHARISMS TYPICALLY *NOT* WELCOMED AND FOSTERED IN PAROCHIAL SETTINGS

The common institutional bias toward maintenance over mission has a downside where charisms are concerned. Pastors and leaders tend to not welcome, to ignore, or even to unconsciously repel certain gifts in a parish setting. Those charisms include:

- Leadership
- Extraordinary Faith
- Celibacy
- Evangelism (*except in youth ministry*)
- Missionary
- Voluntary Poverty
- Prophecy
- Teaching
- Knowledge
- Writing
- Intercessory Prayer
- Healing

I began to grasp this pattern some years ago when I received a call from a man who was in charge of a diaconate formation program. He asked me, "What kind of charisms does a deacon need to have?"

I couldn't think of any charisms excluded by the theology of the diaconate. I suspected that the real issue was elsewhere. So, I asked, "What kind of deacon did your bishop want?" He was very clear: "My bishop wants a man who will recognize when somebody is in distress or needs pastoral care and will take direct personal care of that person himself."

I easily named four or five charisms that fit that kind of job description. But then I added, "I am not aware of any theological reasons why a deacon could not also have a charism of Leadership or Knowledge or Extraordinary Faith." His reply was to the point: "That's not the kind of deacon my bishop wants."

The rejection of certain charisms is seldom that explicit but just as effective in practice. People pick up the subtle cues that that their gift(s) makes other parishioners uncomfortable or are not wanted. If that happens consistently enough, people either bury their gifts to "fit in" or leave for a place where they will be welcomed. Some of our Catholic losses to various Protestant congregations are simply because they welcome and honor charisms that we do not value. People go where their gifts are welcome.

This dynamic is especially critical in light of the challenges we face today. *The charisms typically not welcomed in our parishes include the gifts involved in evangelizing and proclaiming Christ, forming disciples and apostles, and starting new initiatives and movements. These gifts fuel prophetic change and the freedom for unusual, out-of-the-box mission.*

For years, I've had to tell individuals with a probable charism of Leadership that they were going to have to find an exceptional pastor or bishop who would let them do what leaders do: create new mission-centered groups or movements. Pastors with a Leadership charism were also rare, because most parishes were not looking for leaders with missionary vision but for administrators who keep the existing trains well-oiled and running on time.

One of the biggest surprises of my early Catholic life was becoming aware of the isolation of Catholics with the charism of Evangelism. A lay evangelizer might be doing amazing work among "nones" or have brought a dozen spiritual seekers to RCIA, but if he or she was not on a parish committee or working as an usher at the 9:30 a.m. Mass, other parishioners thought of them as marginal. Pastors with a passion for evangelization almost always felt isolated among their brother priests and were considered to be mavericks in their diocese.

All of it made sense once I understood that these charisms were historically associated with religious communities who undertook missionary work outside the stability of a Christendom setting. I began to understand why they were an uncomfortable fit in a parochial setting. The purpose of the parish was seen as providing a benefice for the pastor and a liturgical, sacramental, and catechetical center for the existing Christian community. In Christendom, the parish was hardly ever understood as a serious base for outward-focused apostolic work.

Thank God, the conversation has changed dramatically over the past four or five years in the United States. Now that we have accepted that Christendom has well and truly collapsed in the West, we have to grasp the practical implications of the fact that almost all of our Catholic institutions — including our parishes — stand in true missionary territory. We must learn to recognize and welcome the *ad extra* charisms that God is giving us.

Ad Intra and *Ad Extra*

Charisms that are directed inward toward the building up of the Church can be thought of as "*ad intra*" charisms, while charisms that are directed outward toward the Church's mission in the world could be called "*ad extra*" charisms. Two charisms exercised primarily *within* and whose focus is the Christian community include Pastoring and Prophecy. They are ordered toward building up the Christian community, and to challenging the community to respond to and obey the word of God now.

Conversely, the gift of Evangelism is typically exercised *outside or on the spiritual peripheries of the Christian community*. However, in an era of unevangelized and uncatechized "baptized pagans," those given a charism of Evangelism recognize and seek to address "peripheries" that lie, paradoxically, *within* the Church. Someone with the charism of Evangelism is always asking how to meet people where they are and help them make the rest of the journey to full discipleship to Jesus Christ.

Those charisms most critical to *day-to-day structural maintenance* are Administration and Service (which is why maintenance-minded people love them). Those spiritual gifts most associated with *starting something new* are Leadership and Extraordinary Faith (which is why maintenance-minded Catholics may regard these gifts as off-putting and unnecessary).

Your Local Mileage Will Vary

The charism profile of different parishes, as that of different individuals, will vary. There is no one-size-fits-all set of charisms given to every parish, no standard parish "order" of five charisms of Administration, ten charisms of Service, and six gifts of Encouragement, and so on.

We have been amazed to discover that the distribution of charisms in a given parish is often linked in remarkable ways to the needs of the community into which the parish has been inserted. In one small parish in a famous resort town, we were fascinated to discover that the community had been given an exceptional number of charisms of Hospitality and Evangelism.

On the other hand, we once worked with a magnet parish in a poor urban area. People came to that parish from sixty-five different zip codes, which made sense when we began to explore the community's charisms. The congregation's dominant charisms were Mercy, Prophecy, and Voluntary Poverty (a most exceptional profile). Catholics who had been given those charisms, and identified strongly with the concerns which those charisms addressed, drove many miles to be part of a parish where those gifts were welcomed, honored, and exercised. But the parish community simultaneously felt isolated and rejected by other parishes in their diocese because the needs that the community was passionate about were so different from the diocesan norm.

WHEN PEOPLE START DISCERNING CHARISMS, THEY START DISCERNING VOCATION

Even a single identifiable experience of being used by the Holy Spirit to help someone else in a significant way makes the truth that you were anointed by Christ for the sake of a mission come alive. Many people have told us, "This changes everything: how I understand God and my relationship with God and how I understand the Church."

When you have a lot of people experiencing these "aha" moments of discovery, the idea that ordinary Catholics have something to discern and an apostolic stance toward all of life starts to look normal. A culture where discipleship is normal is a culture where discerning God's call is also normal. And a parish where discerning God's call is normal is one in which many adults will naturally consider possible religious and priestly vocations as well as all manner of secular calls.

A COUPLE OF PRACTICAL NOTES

I am not a professional writer, so the fact that I could provide only the most basic introduction to discerning charisms and the implications for parish life in a book of reasonable length has come as something of a rude awakening. We have learned a great deal in twenty-four years of facilitating discernment that I could not squeeze into this book.

Demand has grown steadily, so we offer Called & Gifted events and training not only around the United States but increasingly around the world. We have trained thousands of pastoral leaders to offer gifts-discernment interviews and facilitate discernment in small groups. Conducting effective individual-gifts interviews involves a fairly sophisticated skill set that needs to be learned in a "live" setting, so I will not attempt to describe it here. If you would like more information about scheduled Called & Gifted-related events, or to talk to a live person about the training and resources that the Institute offers, please visit our website at http://www.siena.org.

THE SHORTEST AND SUREST PATH

I want to end this chapter on a personal note. My first job out of college was a nightmare. I was hired by an organization as a secretary. I'd worked there less than a month when I learned that the head of the organization was secretly planning to resign and was grooming me as his unwitting successor. He had not told anybody he was leaving, and I had absolutely no experience or preparation for the work I was suddenly thrust into when he left shortly thereafter.

The result was dramatic failure. I left the job before they fired me. That was the beginning of a very dark period in my life. I literally came within twenty-five cents of being homeless. I truly felt as though I had been weighed, found wanting, and cast out. I seemed to have no future.

I had already discovered the Dominican parish near campus and made it my "prayer place." I often went there to seek God in my anguish. One day, I happened across a little book in the vestibule that contained a meditation by someone I had never heard of: John Henry Newman. It read, in part:

> God has determined, unless I interfere with his plan, that I should reach that which will be my greatest happiness. He looks on me individually, He calls me by my name, He knows what I can do, what I can best be, what is my greatest happiness, and He means to give it to me.[5]

And it included these electrifying words:

> Therefore I will trust him. Whatever, wherever I am, I can never be thrown away.[6]

Of course, I knew nothing of Newman, nothing of his own struggles as a convert looked upon with suspicion by both Anglicans and his fellow Catholics. But those words went

---

[5] Blessed John Henry Newman, *Meditations and Devotions* (London: Burns and Gates, Ltd., 1964), p. 5.
[6] Ibid., p. 7.

straight to my heart and gave me my first glimmer of hope. I didn't have the money to buy the book, so I left it in the vestibule and later couldn't quite remember the title or the author. It took me years to track down the author of those words and their full context. All I took away was the memory of the words, "I can never be thrown away." Newman's words were still full of power a century after his death. Those words were the light in my darkness.

In the years since, I have had many people of all ages and all walks of life ask similar questions: "Is it too late for me? Have I been thrown away?"

If you don't remember anything else from this book, please remember this: *In Jesus Christ, you can never be thrown away.*

No poverty or misfortune, lack of family, connections, or education; no suffering or failures; no experiences of institutionalized injustice can ultimately thwart God's intention that you should reach that which will be your greatest happiness. As John Donne, the seventeenth-century rector of St. Paul's Cathedral, knew, God "brought light out of darkness, not out of a lesser light; he can bring thy summer out of winter, though thou have no spring."[7]

What does Newman mean by "unless I interfere with his plan"? Basically this: *Only you* can ultimately thwart God's purposes for your life, and *only if you leave him.* Not even your sins can thwart God's redemptive purposes for you, unless you leave him. When you or I sin, we need only to say "I'm sorry" (even if for the millionth time), repent, get back up, and take God's hand again. If you stay with the Father, if you abide in Jesus, he *will* make a way.

---

[7] John Donne, *Sermon for Christmas Day*, 1624, Johann M. Moser, ed., *O Holy Night!: Masterworks of Christmas Poetry* (Manchester, NH: Sophia Institute Press, 1995), p. 9.

I cannot promise that it will be the romantic way that most of us would have preferred. You will probably not make millions by the time you are thirty or become a rock star or IT giant or revel in a perfect family life or whatever you dreamed. Grace is not magic, and the consequences of our choices and the choices of others are real, both for good and ill. But the redemption wrought by Jesus Christ is more powerful than those consequences if we will welcome it into our lives.

God *will* make a way for you to make a difference in the Kingdom if you abide in Jesus. What John Henry Newman wrote about the trustworthiness of God so long ago is still true at this hour in your life:

> God has created me to do Him some definite service; He has committed some work to me which He has not committed to another. I have my mission — I never may know it in this life, but I shall be told it in the next. Somehow I am necessary for His purposes, as necessary in my place as an Archangel in his.... He has not created me for naught. I shall do good, I shall do his work; I shall be an angel of peace, a preacher of truth in my own place, while not intending it, if I do but keep His commandments and serve Him in my calling.
>
> Therefore I will trust Him. Whatever, wherever I am, I can never be thrown away.[8]

Your vocation is your shortest and surest earthly path to your ultimate eternal happiness with God. It is also the way through which you will have the privilege of helping many others reach their ultimate happiness. Your charisms are an

---

[8] Newman, *Meditations and Devotions*, pp. 6-7.

important part of identifying that path. Your gifts are both clues to your personal vocation and supernaturally empowered tools that God has given you so that you can fruitfully accomplish your mission.

The great work to which God calls you — calls all of us — awaits. Let us undertake the obedience of discernment so that we may bear abundant fruit — fruit that will last and bless untold generations to come.

CHAPTER 10

Facing Outward

"Go, therefore, and make disciples of all nations, baptizing them in the name of the Father, and of the Son, and of the Holy Spirit, teaching them to observe all that I have commanded you. And behold, I am with you always, until the end of the age."

MATTHEW 28:19-20

A friend of mine who works in an evangelizing parish in the Upper Midwest shared this story with me the other day:

One of our teenagers invited a friend to attend a youth event at the parish. Our visitor, "Rachel," had no faith upbringing, but when she stepped into the sanctuary and heard the music, she was deeply stirred and felt peace that she had never experienced. So, Rachel joined the teen choir and then got involved in the youth ministry group. It was there that Rachel encountered Jesus and was supported and mentored as a disciple and baptized. She started to manifest the charism of Mercy and began going out to serve the poor with another friend from the parish.

No one at the parish is surprised that Rachel is discerning a vocation to religious life as I write this. In *Becoming a Parish of Intentional Disciples*, Bobby Vidal writes:

The overarching goal of parish renewal is this: to create a community where it is easier for individuals to become intentional disciples, live as intentional disciples, and make intentional disciples.[1]

Bobby created a list of fifteen typical changes that occur and fruits that are borne as a parish moves from being maintenance-driven to being mission-driven. He uses the list as a springboard to help parish leaders recognize and tell the story of what God was doing in their midst. His list begins like this:

Maintenance	Mission
1. Getting parishioners involved in the many events, activities, and experiences of the parish.	1. Helping all people to encounter Jesus Christ and experience conversion through parish events and activities and also in life and events outside the parish.
2. Recruiting and training individuals to take on leadership roles.	2. Forming individuals in discerning their individual charisms and their God-given vocation.
3. Getting parishioners to commit to different tasks that would have them give more time, talent, and treasure to the parish.	3. Helping individuals commit their entire life to Jesus and then to live out that commitment daily.

---

[1] Bobby Vidal, "Intentional Disciples: Bearing Spiritual Fruit That Sustains," in *Becoming a Parish of Intentional Disciples*, p. 70.

Maintenance	Mission
4. Sustaining the current structures of the parish, thereby maintaining the number of people in the parish.	4. Sustaining a culture of discipleship, thereby creating a path to discipleship that is owned, supported, and sustained by the whole parish community.

What kind of fruit could be borne in a parish that has created a path to discipleship that is owned, supported, and sustained by the whole community? The leaders of a different disciple-making parish shared this story with me a few months ago:

"Brian," a young Catholic guy who didn't attend Mass and spent a lot of time in bars drinking heavily, felt moved to go back to Mass once after 9/11. As he stood in the back of the sanctuary, he heard the youth ministry team asking for volunteers to serve the teens of the parish and take them to heaven. Brian was so moved by that announcement that he volunteered on the spot and his involvement in youth ministry became the catalyst of a whole new life. He experienced a major conversion, was discipled in the parish, grew spiritually by leaps and bounds, and then discerned a call to the priesthood. Now newly ordained, Brian says that hearing that announcement to come and serve the youth of the parish and take them to heaven was the spark that God used to lead him to the priesthood.

Rachel's and Brian's experiences are great examples of how an evangelizing parish that is prepared to do so can help a lapsed

Catholic or even a stranger with no faith background move from *seeker* to *disciple*, and then become an emerging *apostle*.

PARISH CULTURE MATTERS

We have observed over the years that the cultural norm in place in most parishes unintentionally *suppresses* and *impedes* the spiritual growth and conversion of many. By cultural norm, I don't mean the parish mission statement but the unspoken assumptions about what is and is not right, appropriate, and "normal" that governs the community's behavior. Cultural norms don't have to be put into words to be powerful.

It is pretty easy to know when you violate the unwritten rules of any group. People are startled, become uneasy, or even afraid or angry. In my early days as a Catholic, I was always asking the wrong question, and reducing cradle Catholics to incredulous silence. Many of my problem questions were related to a single overriding concern: Wasn't the Catholic faith supposed to change people's lives?

When I started graduate school, the issues became more global. When I did a paper on RCIA, I made an appointment with the local diocesan director of RCIA. I wondered aloud: Did parishes keep in touch with those received at Easter and monitor their Christian growth? Did they follow up when a new Catholic stopped coming? The director gave me what I had started to think of as "the look" and responded that it would be invasive of the spiritual privacy of the newly baptized to keep in touch.

I finally pulled a real whopper. I naively blurted out, "Was "Father 'X' effective?" at a parish committee meeting. When the woman across the table from me erupted in rage at my presumption, I finally understood. I was violating another one of those deeply held Catholic norms that wasn't in the *Catechism* but all "real" Catholics instinctively knew: *Never ask if you are being effective, never ask if you are having the desired spiritual impact.* I sat through the rest of that meeting in stunned silence, thinking, "I will never, never, never-ever be Catholic enough. I will never understand Catholics if I live to be one hundred." The irony is that the priest in question was none other than Father Michael Sweeney, O.P., with whom I eventually founded the Catherine of Siena Institute. It turned out that he was asking similar questions!

We have found that the typical overall cultural norm of an average diocesan parish is at the earliest and most passive threshold of pre-discipleship: *trust.* This is not, of course, true of every parish or every single member of such parishes. There are a sizable number of Catholics embedded in our parishes who are amazing disciples and even saints (we have met them!). But what you often hear from mature disciples is how isolated and even rejected they feel because they have moved beyond the communal spiritual norm.

AN ENCOURAGING SPIRITUAL CULTURE

In contrast, the *average* spiritual norm of a typical evangelical congregation is early discipleship. It is certainly *not* because they are smarter or spiritual geniuses, or that God loves them more. But the overall culture of a typical evangelical church is centered around making a personal response to the challenge that Jesus issued to his earliest followers: "Come after me, and I will make you fishers of men" (Matthew 4:19). Not every evangelical is a disciple. Far from it. But the functioning *norm* in most of those communities is early — not mature — discipleship. As a result, evangelical congregations strongly encourage everyone they encounter to take the first step of discipleship.

It is also vital to note that there are Catholic parishes where the culture is far beyond the threshold of trust. In the past five years, we have been delighted to find that many parishes are deliberately setting out to move from a maintenance cultural norm to one of missionary discipleship. Most are still in the early stages. The good news is that, as a parish culture becomes more accepting and supportive of intentional discipleship, it becomes easier and faster for more parishioners to make their journey through the thresholds and become disciples. It is like a feedback loop: as discipleship becomes the center of parish life, the easier it is for people to become disciples. Meanwhile, disciples change a congregation's spiritual culture just through their emerging questions and concerns — so the more disciples there are, the faster the culture changes.

RETAIL EVANGELIZATION

I once heard a shrewd Dominican pastor observe that because of our numbers, American pastors and parish leaders tend to do religion "wholesale, not retail." We move hundreds through the sacramental prep and various catechetical and service programs, while telling ourselves that we do not have the luxury of attending to God's grace at work in individuals. But "retail" — the saving work of God in an individual human heart — is the end for which the parish and the pastoral office exist. It is what gives "wholesale" its purpose and meaning.

Our institutional trellises exist to support the fruit-bearing Vine — which is Jesus and his people. Without individual and communal conversion, very little fruit is borne, regardless of the structures you put in place. *Parish structures do not bear fruit; they support fruit-bearers.*

Without an absolute, non-negotiable, vision of the human fruit we are supposed to bear, we cannot discern what kinds of pastoral structures we really need. We will not be able to recognize where we are failing, and we won't be able to identify obstacles. We cannot revise our pastoral practices to foster more abundant fruit-bearing unless our purpose is clear from the beginning and always the criteria by which we measure everything we do.

At this moment in our history, we need to build a parish-literate missionary band of evangelizers whose primary work is to help individuals and families become mature disciples and fruit-bearing apostles. It does not have to be a glacial process. *In a highly supportive parish environment, many people can make the journey from seeker to a fruit-bearing emerging apostle in one to two years.*

Our dream at the Catherine of Siena Institute is to enable, not just a few, but *thousands* of ordinary Catholics in our larger parishes to acquire the evangelical ears and eyes to recognize somebody in whom the Holy Spirit is at work and who is beginning to move through the thresholds of pre-discipleship. We dream of parishes filled with skilled evangelizing companions who can understand, support, and walk with people of any background who are on this journey. When this kind of personal support is available in the parish, it reinforces and greatly magnifies the impact of larger scale evangelizing initiatives such as homilies, parish missions, evangelizing courses or retreats, or RCIA.

To help make that dream come true, the Institute has developed a formation process that we call *Ananias Training*, named after Ananias, the layman who first supported St. Paul after his dramatic encounter with Jesus on the road to Damascus. Ananias Training is not spiritual direction but a much more elementary formation that teaches the skills of listening evangelism and how to speak to adults in the early stages of trust, curiosity, and openness. Ananias Training includes learning how to recognize the thresholds of pre-discipleship, how to have threshold conversations, how to tell your own story, and how to tell Jesus' Great Story.[2]

THE PARISH: MISSION OUTWARD

The missional potential of our 221,740 parishes[3] inserted into the neighborhoods of the world is enormous. Pope Francis summed up our situation very well:

> The parish is not an outdated institution; precisely because it possesses great flexibility, it can assume quite different contours depending on the openness and missionary creativity of the pastor and the community.[4]

What could the larger impact of a local congregation filled with "missionary creativity" look like? In famously secular New York City, there is an evangelical community at the center of an emerging Christian renaissance from which Catholic evangelizers could learn much: Redeemer Presbyterian Church. I've been following their progress for a few years now. Even though they are not Catholic, the congregation is living and applying significant aspects of our own Catholic theology of evangelization in remarkably fruitful ways.

---

[2]   For more information about Ananias Training, go to https://www.siena.org/ananias-training.

[3]   Center for Applied Research in the Apostolate, "Frequently Requested Church Statistics," 2014 (online http://cara.georgetown.edu/frequently-requested-church-statistics/, as of May 5, 2017).

[4]   Pope Francis, *Evangelii Gaudium*, 28.

Their mission statement reads:

> As a church of Jesus Christ, Redeemer exists to help
> build a great city for all people through a movement of
> the gospel that brings personal conversion, community
> formation, social justice, and cultural renewal to New
> York City and, through it, to the world.[5]

Redeemer began in 1989 as a small group of Christians
meeting to pray about starting a new congregation to reach
young adult professionals. When senior pastor Tim Keller
joined them later that year, New York City was the least religious
city in the United States. Less than 1 percent of New Yorkers
attended what Redeemer would call a "gospel teaching" church.

A lot has changed in the intervening twenty-eight years.
In 2017, 9,000 regularly attend Redeemer's three linked but
independent congregations in different parts of Manhattan.
Redeemer is part of a much larger network of evangelizing
congregations and initiatives in New York City that has begun
to change the spiritual culture of the whole region and has
sparked an urban movement. A recent survey has found that
five times more center-city New Yorkers living in Manhattan,
Brooklyn, and Queens now attend a variety of "gospel-teaching"
churches than did in 1989. Redeemer's current goal is to see the
current 5 percent figure rise to 15 percent in the next ten years
— possibly reaching a cultural tipping point.[6]

Between 2001 and 2011, Barna Research also found significant growth in Christian practice in the New York media

---

[5] Redeemer Presbyterian Church, *Vision and Values* (online at http://www
.redeemer.com/learn/about_us/vision_and_values, as of May 5, 2017).

[6] *Rise: A Vision That Will Take All of Us*, Mission Investor Guide (online at
http://rise.redeemer.com/wp-content/uploads/2016/03/RISEBOOK
-website2.pdf, as of May 5, 2017).

market (which includes the northern half of New Jersey, south-ern-most New York state, and bits of Connecticut and Penn-sylvania). Weekly church attendance in the area is up 15 per-cent (increasing to 46 percent of those surveyed), and there has been a significant drop in those who had not attended church in six months (down 8 percent, dropping to 34 percent of those surveyed). Barna found that most of the change has happened since 2004 and was *not* a result of 9/11.

> Whatever the combination of causes, the residents of the New York City region are more spiritually active, more likely to be "churched," and more committed to Christ than they were a decade ago.[7]

The *New York Times* has reported on this trend as well:

> The recent growth of evangelicalism is noticeable but difficult to quantify. According to Mr. Carnes, there are 1.2 million to 1.6 million evangelicals in the city, which he said was an increase of about 22 percent since 2000. To arrive at the estimate, he synthesized several studies, including the American Values Atlas and work by the Pew Research Center, and culled information from his journal's database of 6,600 churches.[8]

Part of this growth is due to immigration. A great many of the new Christians in the heart of the city are not Anglos. But

---

[7] Barna Research, *Barna Study Explores Faith in New York Since 9-11*, August 29, 2011 (online at https://www.barna.com/research/barna-study-explores -faith-in-new-york-since-9-11/, as of May 5, 2017).

[8] Liz Robbins, "An Evangelical Revival in the Heart of New York," *New York Times*, July 9, 2015 (online at http://www.nytimes.com/2015/07/10 /nyregion/central-park-festival-to-highlight-new-yorks-vibrant-evangelical -movement.html, as of May 5, 2017).

the majority of Redeemer Presbyterian's membership is made up of "young urban professionals" — that is, those most alienated from Christianity — and that population is primarily Anglo and Asian. There is talk of a possible "Great Awakening" in evangelical circles in New York these days. What can Catholic evangelizers learn from this movement?

Do You Live in Christendom?

When Redeemer Presbyterian was founded, everyone involved *knew* that they did not live in Christendom. But an important question for Catholic evangelizers who live in the rest of the country is "Do I live in Christendom — or at least in some fragment of it?" Tim Keller writes:

> [I]n the United States there is still a heartland with remnants of the old Christendom society. There the informal public culture, though not the formal public institutions, still stigmatizes non-Christian beliefs and behavior. There is a fundamental schism in American cultural, political, and economic life. There's the quicker-growing, economically vibrant ... morally relativist, urban-oriented, culturally adventuresome, sexually polymorphous, and ethnically diverse nation.... And there's the small-town, nuclear-family, religiously oriented, white-centric other America, [with] ... its diminishing cultural and economic force.... [T]wo countries. In conservative regions, it is still possible to see people professing faith and the church growing without becoming missional.[9]

---

[9] Tim Keller, *The Missional Church*, June 2001, p. 1, 2 (online at http://dashhouse.com/wp-content/uploads/2016/07/MissionalChurch-Keller.pdf, as of May 5, 2017).

Many places in the Deep South, where I grew up, would still qualify as part of this "informal cultural Christendom." But in places like Seattle, New York, or London, Christendom no longer exists. Keller makes a critical observation:

> Most traditional evangelical churches can win to Christ only people who are temperamentally traditional and conservative. As Wolff notes, however, this is a shrinking market, and eventually evangelical churches ensconced in the declining, remaining enclaves of Christendom will have to learn how to become missional. If they do not, they will decline or die.[10]

Here in the United States, therefore, we need to ask, "Is the community to which God has called me still part of cultural Christendom? If not, how does that change how we must evangelize? What fragments of the old Christian moral and spiritual consensus do I, as a believing Catholic, still share with the people around me?" For instance, one community may resonate with the Church's teaching on solidarity but have great hostility to her teaching on life issues. Different places will have different fragments better preserved than others.

LOCAL THEOLOGICAL VISION: MIDDLEWARE

To evangelize effectively in our generation, it is not sufficient for us to master the Church's Tradition and then share it with those who are already inclined toward it. If we simply wait for the minority who are naturally and culturally inclined toward Christian values to come to us, we can look forward to continued dramatic decline. The Church is calling us to go out into the

---

[10] Ibid., p. 2.

world to bring Christ to those whose worldview is dramatically different, while remaining faithful to all the Church teaches. How is this possible?

If we think of our doctrine as "hardware" and our pastoral practices and programs as "software," there is a software layer between the two that knowledgeable computer professionals call "middleware." Middleware is essentially a software layer that lies between your hardware and operating system and your software applications. For instance, middleware would connect your database with your web server. In a similar way, theological middleware can help us bridge the even greater divide between the Church's teaching and the mind-set of those to whom God is sending us.

Tim Keller points out that we need evangelizing middleware — a *local* theological vision — to be effective evangelizers in our time. This means we need

> ... a well-conceived vision for how to bring the gospel to bear on the particular cultural setting and historical moment. This is something more practical than just doctrinal beliefs but much more theological than "how-to steps" for carrying out a particular ministry. Once this vision is in place, with its emphases and values, it leads church leaders to make good decisions on how to ... disciple, evangelize, serve and engage culture in their field of ministry....[11]

St. Paul expressed the same idea like this:

> To the Jews I became like a Jew to win over Jews; to those under the law I became like one under the law —

---

[11] Tim Keller, *Center Church: Doing Balanced, Gospel-Centered Ministry in Your City* (Grand Rapids, MI: Zondervan, 2012), p. 17.

though I myself am not under the law — to win over
those under the law. To those outside the law I became
like one outside the law — though I am not outside
God's law but within the law of Christ — to win over
those outside the law. To the weak I became weak, to
win over the weak. I have become all things to all, to
save at least some. (1 Corinthians 9:20-22)

Middleware corresponds roughly to what Catholics call
"pastoral" or "practical" theology. A book like *Forming Intentional
Disciples* is a kind of middleware, originally written to help
American Catholic leaders grasp the realities of our time and
the new post-modern culture in which we proclaim Christ. (The
fact that so many Catholics outside the United States found my
book spoke to their situation came as a big surprise. Now I
know that Catholic leaders seem to find *Forming Intentional
Disciples* useful wherever Western culture has had a significant
impact — including in non-Western countries.) Missiology is a
specific kind of middleware or pastoral theology that is focused
on mission outward beyond the Christian community.

Fruitful evangelization is the result of the great Catholic
"both/and." We must hold, believe, pray, and think deeply about
the fullness of the Church's teaching. *And at the same time, we
must listen to, pray, and meditate deeply on the cultural, emotional,
and intellectual landscape of our particular community*. It is the
only way to generate a local theological vision that enables us
to make good decisions about the specific practices that will
foster fruitful disciple-making *in our setting*. For instance,
when members of the Forming Intentional Disciples Facebook
Forum ask, "Should my parish use this evangelizing retreat or
that course?" the most helpful answer is often "It depends."

In the past few years, there has been a welcome flurry of new
tools and "best practices," but our tendency is still to presume

that tools work equally well, independent of the setting in which they are used. A friend tells us about some great evangelizing retreat that worked in an evangelical campus ministry in urban Boston and, in our rush to do something, we just grab it off the shelf and plunk it down in the middle of a long-established Catholic parish in Boise. And then we wonder why it is such a struggle. Keller describes the problem this way:

> [M]any ministers take up programs and practices of ministry that fit well with neither their doctrinal beliefs nor their cultural context. They adopt popular methods that are essentially "glued on" from the outside — alien to the church's theology or setting (or both!). And when that happens, we find a lack of fruitfulness. These ministers don't change people's lives with the church and don't reach people in their city. Why not? Because the programs did not grow naturally out of reflection on both the gospel and the distinctness of their surrounding culture.[12]

We need to do both if we are going to make disciples, not just offer more one-size-fits-all programs for ever smaller numbers.

Facing Outward

One of the core values of Redeemer Presbyterian is what they call "outward face." Outward face means maintaining an awareness at all times of how our assumptions, practices, language, and interactions look to the non-believers who are watching:

---

[12] Ibid., pp. 16-17.

Redeemer has always sought to be a place where doubters felt their questions were noticed and taken seriously.... Sermons should be preached, and public events (even most small groups) conducted as if non-Christians were present, overhearing what we are saying. *We must constantly keep in mind what it is like to not believe.*... It is crucial that a large percentage of Christians come into Redeemer and think, "I wish my non-Christian friend could hear this."[13]

We are not used to thinking about *what it is like to not believe* because, until a couple generations ago, the majority of American Catholics lived in parish-centered immigrant communities — a solid Christendom setting. But increasingly, most of our communities and institutions are located outside the remnants of Christendom. We all have agnostics and atheists, nones, and seekers in our lives, families, and parishes. It is time to ask ourselves, "What would a Catholic parish with a true outward face look like?" What would have to change if my parish were to become a place where doubters felt their questions were taken seriously? What would it take to make my parish a place where large numbers of parishioners would spontaneously say, "I wish my non-believing or non-Catholic friend could hear and be part of this."

A DIOCESE FACING OUTWARD

What could happen if an entire Catholic diocese, from the bishop to catechists, committed to evangelization and mis-

---

[13] Redeemer Presbyterian Church, *Vision and Values*, 7. Outward Face (online at http://www.redeemer.com/learn/about_us/vision_and_values, as of May 5, 2017).

sion outward together? We are about to find out because a few American dioceses have set out on that exciting quest in different ways. Let me share a little of what has happened so far in one of those dioceses: Lansing, Michigan.

Like most American dioceses over the past few decades, Lansing has seen a steady decline in Mass attendance, baptisms, confirmations, marriages, and parish registration. For instance, Mass attendance declined 23 percent in Lansing between 2007 and 2015,[14] and the number of infant baptisms dropped 36 percent between 2006 and 2014.[15]

For a whole diocese to go on mission together, pastors and leaders need to share a common vision. In 2010, the first Parish Engagement Report for the diocese was produced for Bishop Earl Boyea, making clear the size of the problem. In response, the bishop appointed a task force on engagement and discipleship. In April 2012, Bishop Boyea promulgated a pastoral letter, *Go and Announce the Gospel of the Lord*. Bishop Boyea's challenge to his community was clear:

> Many today do not know Jesus. Let us evangelize our world! There are sisters and brothers, family members and friends who have left the Church. Let us re-engage them in the life of the Body of Christ! We cannot do this unless we ourselves are converted more fully to the Lord Jesus. Let us be his disciples![16]

The bishop's pastoral letter identified three categories of people to whom the Church's evangelization efforts were to

---

[14] Patrick O'Brien, *Parish Engagement Report 2016* (Catholic Diocese of Lansing, 2016), p. 4.

[15] Ibid., p. 11.

[16] Bishop Earl Boyea, *Go and Announce the Gospel of the Lord*, April 5, 2012, p. 7 (online at https://lansingdiocese.faithdev.org/sites/default/files/2017-03/PastoralLetter2012_0.pdf, as of May 5, 2017).

be directed: (1) practicing Catholics, (2) Catholics who don't practice their faith or have left the Church, and (3) spiritually open or seeking non-Catholics and non-believers. Every parish council in the diocese was given a kit containing the report, a study guide, recommendations, resources, and a copy of a parish evaluation inventory. Every parish council was asked to create a parish plan for evangelization and discipleship.

Bishop Boyea began with prayer. He designated the seventeen months from Friday, August 3, 2012, to Monday, December 9, 2013, as a "long year" of prayer "for the spiritual renewal of our diocese, for an outpouring of the Holy Spirit upon us, and for the salvation of our souls, those of our lost sheep and, indeed, of the whole world."[17] That summer, he hired Craig Pohl as director of the New Evangelization. In 2014, the bishop announced that three diocesan assemblies were to be held two years apart, each assembly focusing upon the challenge of reaching one of these three groups.

Four and a half years into this process, I received a delighted e-mail from Craig Pohl, who had just seen the 2016 October Mass attendance count. The first significant signs of a spiritual tipping point were becoming visible. Parish registrations had gone up the previous year, and the number of infant baptisms had held steady for the first time in years. *In a single year (2015-2016), the decline in diocesan Mass attendance had slowed nearly 50 percent, and the number of growing parishes had doubled from twelve to twenty-four.* Ten of those parishes had experienced double-digit growth in Mass attendance. Growing parishes were at the center of the positive change:

> The slowing of overall declines in Mass attendance across the diocese is not due to an improvement among declining parishes. Those that continue to decline are

---

[17] Ibid, p. 18.

doing so at the same rate. The improvement we are seeing is mostly due to the increase in growing parishes.[18]

As Craig put it:

> There's no mistaking it, a positive change is happening
> here. We considered all the other possible scenarios for
> why this might be happening and at this time we can
> only point to the New Evangelization efforts.[19]

The Institute has worked in the Lansing diocese during
the past few years, so we have been eagerly tracking Lansing's
process and cheering them on. But the possibilities really came
alive for me when I met newly ordained Father James Mangan
and he told me about his work in the Catholic Community of
Flint.[20]

Flint has gotten a lot of bad press lately for dangerous
drinking water, but that does not begin to exhaust Flint's
problems. It is a classic Rust Belt scenario: the city's population
has dropped to half of what it was in the mid-1960s. Many
people have been unemployed for so long that they are not
counted as unemployed anymore. Forty-two percent of the
population has an income at or below the poverty line, and drug
addiction has skyrocketed. Flint has made the list of the most
dangerous cities in the United States every year for the past
decade.

In its heyday, Flint was at the center of the American
automotive industry and a Catholic stronghold with twelve
Catholic high schools and fourteen Catholic parishes. All but
one high school and eight parishes are closed now. Father Tom

---

[18] O'Brien, *Parish Engagement Report 2016*, p. 2.
[19] Private e-mail correspondence with Craig Pohl, January 13, 2017.
[20] http://www.flintcatholic.org/, as of May 5, 2017.

Firestone pastors what is called the Catholic Community of Flint, with the assistance of Father James and two other young priest assistants, a priest chaplain for the high school, and a deacon. The community includes four parishes with a total of over 1,500 families, a high school with 700 students, a hospital, a prayer/retreat center, Catholic Charities, and a life-skills and workplace training center run by two women religious. While the population of Flint is nearly 56 percent black, the Catholic community is still overwhelmingly white, although there is one African-American and one Hispanic parish in Flint. One hopeful sign is that two of the community's parishes experienced double-digit growth in Mass attendance last year.

Father James has served in the community for a year and a half and told me that when a priest is assigned in Flint, his real assignment is to the entire community, not just a specific parish. The priests rotate so they can have a more unified liturgical and preaching approach. Father James said:

> The heart of what is new is rethinking how we do local church. The old parochial model is not working here in Flint. Our parishes are crumbling. The idea that you can establish a community based on consumption doesn't work in Flint. That is a suburban model, a model of Church which is more based on going to the place where you are "fed," where the priests or the music fits my needs.

> We are surrounded by fairly large, suburban parishes, ten-fifteen minutes out. We could have merged all the parishes here or closed the parishes and told people to go to the suburbs. Why do we remain in Flint? Because the Church has a responsibility to be present, particularly where there is great need, great suffering, and lots of non-Catholics. There are all kinds of people

out there suffering without Christ. We are only here for mission.

Many of our people commute to attend Mass. We are dying to the idea of just going to the parish where you live and dying to the idea that our primary allegiance as a Catholic is to the parish rather than to the larger Catholic community in this place, in this mission field. We encourage people to go to the parish where they can serve, can be on mission, where their gifts or interests have an avenue for expression. Each of the four parishes has their own approach to outreach, and we want people to go to the place where they can contribute to the mission of that site.

Our main hub is St. John Vianney, where we have a school. We have moved all our religious education to the school and parish. It is now our educational hub where our goal is to form child disciples and build bridges. We are revamping religious education in the school so it is aimed at initiating children and families into relationship with Jesus in midst of the Church. Our school has been our most successful vehicle for evangelizing someone who is culturally distant from the Catholic faith.

St. Mary Parish is in a very poor area and a Catholic Worker community is beginning to take shape there. St. Matthew is the center for our mission to the downtown community, the university, students, and business people. We are considering reaching out through concerts and a speaker series, a coffee shop, and the arts. St. Michael Parish is the oldest parish in the county and across the street from Catholic Charities. We are hoping to get parishioners more involved with Catholic Charities.

Father James's final observations moved me to dream again:

> We are also dreaming of creating little neighborhoods
> or homes to get into the veins of the city and to facili-
> tate a greater sense of community among Catholics. We
> are thinking about community life — incarnate evan-
> gelization — and the need for Catholic leaders to have
> community with each other. We just had a meeting
> with thirty people: business people, young families, stu-
> dents, Catholic Workers and proposed the idea of pur-
> chasing a house. It could serve as a house of hospitality
> for leaders, a place for people working in many different
> areas of the parish and city, a center from which you can
> pivot.

What will the Holy Spirit do if we spend more time
with one another and pray with each other?[21]

What could the Holy Spirit do through us if hundreds of
our parishes were filled with fruit-bearing missionary disciples
who are deliberately entering the veins of our neighborhoods
and cities to bring Jesus Christ to the world? Jesus promised,

> "If you remain in me and my words remain in you, ask
> for whatever you want and it will be done for you. By
> this is my Father glorified, that you bear much fruit and
> become my disciples." (John 15:7-8)

---

[21] Personal interview with Father James Mangan, December 17, 2016.